T0162128

CLUNY

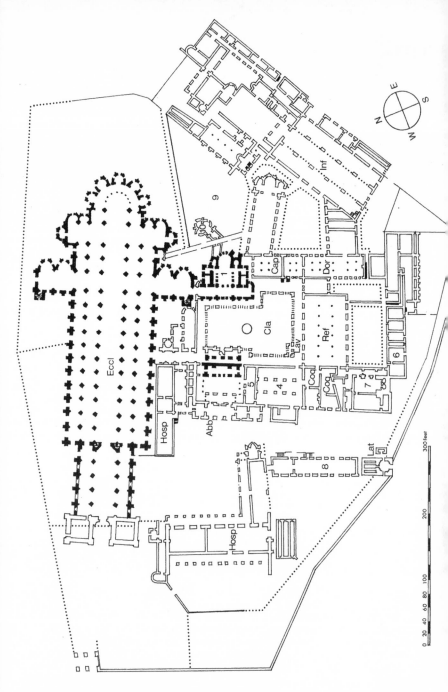

Plan of Cluny in the twelfth century. Eccl: the third church, Cluny III; 1 and 2: remnants of the second church, Cluny II; Cla: cloister; 9: cemetery; 10: cemetery chapel; Cap: chapter house; Dor: dormitory; Inf: infirmary; Lav: lavabo, ceremonial wash place; Ref: refectory; 6: workshops; 7: bakery; Coq: kitchen; 4: storehouse; 5: almonry; Abb: abbot's lodging; Hosp: guest house; 8: stables; Lat: latrine

CLUNY

IN SEARCH OF GOD'S
LOST EMPIRE

Edwin Mullins

BlueBridge

Jacket design by Stefan Killen Design

Cover art top by Archives départementales de Saône-et-Loire (image Cluny 2 Fi 1/83)

Cover art bottom by Art Resource, New York (Eve, Romanesque relief.
Cathedral St. Lazare, Autun, France)

Published in Great Britain by Signal Books Limited, Oxford.

Library of Congress Cataloging-in-Publication Data
Mullins, Edwin B.
Cluny : in search of God's lost empire / Edwin Mullins.
p. cm.
Includes bibliographical references and index.
ISBN 1-933346-00-0
1. Cluny (Benedictine abbey) 2. Monastic and religious life—France—Cluny.
3. Cluny (France)—Church history. I. Title.

BX2615.C63M85 2006
271'. 1404443—dc22
2006014402

Published in North America by
B l u e B r i d g e
An imprint of
United Tribes Media Inc.
240 West 35th Street, Suite 500
New York, NY 10001

www.bluebridgebooks.com

Printed in the United States of America

10 9 8 7 6 5 4 3 2 1

CONTENTS

I. The Long Shadow of the Past   *1*

II. A Hunting Lodge in a Secluded Valley   *13*

III. The Stonemasons from Italy   *25*

IV. A White Mantle of Churches   *37*

V. Hugh the Great   *59*

VI. Spanish Excursions   *69*

VII. Power and Politics   *79*

VIII. Rural Peace . . . and Holy War   *93*

IX. Looking towards England   *103*

X. The Greatest Church in Christendom   *115*

XI. Daily Life at Cluny   *129*

XII. Vanitas Vanitatis   *145*

XIII. Peter the Venerable   *155*

XIV. Battling Bernard of Clairvaux   *167*

XV. Henry the King and Henry the Bishop   *183*

XVI. Héloïse and Abelard   *193*

XVII. Genius in Stone   *207*

XVIII. Decline and Fall   *221*

Bibliography   237

Index   241

List of Illustrations   247

For Anne,

my love

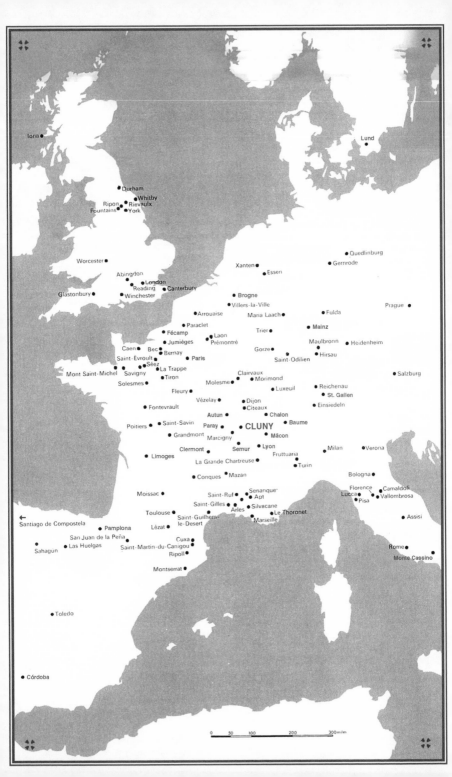

Iona

Lund

Durham
Whitby
Ripon • Rievaulx
Fountains • York

Quedlinburg
Gernrode

Worcester

Xanten
Essen

Abingdon
London
Reading • Canterbury
Glastonbury
Winchester

Brogne
Villers-la-Ville
Arrouaise
Maria Laach
Fulda
Prague

Paraclet
Fécamp
Laon
Trier
Mainz

Jumièges
Prémontré
Maulbronn
Heidenheim

Caen • Bec
Bernay
Paris
Gorze
Saint-Odilien
Hirsau

Saint-Évroult
Sées
La Trappe

Mont Saint-Michel
Savigny
Clairvaux
Salzburg

Solesmes
Tiron
Molesme • Morimond
Luxeuil
Reichenau
St. Gallen

Fleury
Vézelay
Dijon
Cîteaux
Einsiedeln

Fontevrault
Autun
Chalon

Poitiers • Saint-Savin
Paray
CLUNY
Baume

Grandmont
Marcigny
Mâcon

Clermont
Semur
Lyon
Milan
Verona

Limoges
La Grande Chartreuse
Fruttuaria

Turin
Bologna

Conques • Mazan

Moissac
Saint-Ruf
Senanque
Apt
Florence
Camaldoli
Lucca
Vallombrosa
Pisa

Saint-Gilles
Silvacane
Arles
Le Thoronet
Toulouse
Saint-Guilhem-
Marseille
Assisi
le-Desert

Santiago de Compostela
Lézat
Pamplona

San Juan de la Peña
Cuxa

Sahagun • Las Huelgas
Saint-Martin-du-Canigou
Rome
Ripoll
Monte Cassino

Montserrat

Toledo

Córdoba

0   50   100   200   300 miles

The Long Shadow of the Past

Bare ruin'd choirs, where late the sweet birds sang.
Shakespeare, Sonnet 73

 For five hundred years the abbey church of Cluny was the largest house of God in Christendom, demoted to second place only when St. Peter's in Rome was rebuilt in the sixteenth century, and made—deliberately—just a few feet longer.

Today Cluny is a hollow shell filled by the wind and by our curiosity over what was once here. Yet listen carefully and we can hear the echoes of an extraordinary past. A thousand years ago this now-shattered place in southern Burgundy made an impact on the Christian world more profound and more enduring than that of any pope or emperor, or any ruling monarch of the day including the kings of France and England. Cluny's abbots were as influential as any president, statesman, or business leader in our own times. Wielding immense political power, backed by unmatched moral stature, they were men who saw their star and followed it wherever it might lead. They inherited a Europe that lay in ruins and proceeded to rebuild it, laying many of the foundations of Christian culture and civilization. For more than two centuries Cluny was the spiritual heart of Christianity.

In itself it was no more than a small, enclosed world—an abbey behind walls—yet its shadow reached out to the most distant corners of the continent, and even beyond. One of the great reforming popes of the eleventh century, Urban II, formerly a monk here, wrote of Cluny that it "shines as another sun over the earth, so that it is more fitting to apply to it the words of our Lord, 'You are the light of the world.'"

Not many institutions in history have been able to claim that kind of fame and brilliance. So, what of Cluny today?

It can fairly be described as a vast puzzle most of whose clues are missing. Its sufferings over the centuries have been legion, some of them self-inflicted, the majority of them not. Cluny first fell victim to the French religious wars of the seventeenth century, then more disastrously to the Revolutionary mob in the late eighteenth, though long before either of these events the abbey had been growing fat on its own wealth and self-importance, and had become ripe for attack. Finally, and terminally, the place, by now empty, became a victim of the French anticlerical authorities in the wake of the Revolution. As the eighteenth century died, so did Cluny: the abbey and its great church were auctioned off as if the place was just another disused pile of rubble. The successful bidder in this black comedy was a consortium of three citizens of nearby Mâcon who proceeded to sell off the whole place stone by stone, year by year, profit by profit, until in the 1820s a small conscience twitched in the corridors of power, and enough was declared to be enough. But by this time all that was left is the little we now see.

Except—not quite. The past eighty years have witnessed a number of dedicated attempts to rescue and painstakingly restore what managed to escape the plunder of those three grasping citizens of Mâcon. As a result, one can almost say that the vast ghost of Cluny has been brought back to life—or at least that its long shadow is now there for us to peer at, and to explore.

Cluny today is a small provincial town of four thousand people, in the *département* of Saône-et-Loire. The town of Beaune, at the heart of Burgundy's famous vineyards, lies about fifty miles to the north, while Lyon, one of France's largest cities, is about fifty miles to the south. The high-speed TGV train line connecting Paris, Lyon, and Marseille cuts through the rolling hills just outside Cluny.

The search for the Cluny of the past has to begin, appropriately enough, with the monumental stone gateway, which was once the ceremonial entrance to the abbey, and most of which survives. Formerly part of the western wall, it dates from the twelfth century, at the height of Cluny's glory, and it was modeled on the Roman gates of Autun, the Emperor Augustus's city of *Augustodunum* which lies some forty miles to the north, and which also survive. Here is an introduction to the place that tells us immediately that a feeling for Roman grandeur lay at the very center of Cluny's vision.

From here onwards it becomes a journey signposted by relics—sometimes moving, sometimes sad, sometimes tinged with indignity. A pair of massive rectangular towers, known as Les Barabans, originally guarded the western end of the abbey church. These survive, though it takes an effort of the imagination to recognize them since the upper levels were long ago torn away and one of the towers rebuilt as an apartment. The actual approach to the church, leading east from the ceremonial gateway, is a long slope now cleared of masonry except for a broad flight of steps with a steep ramp on either side. You then enter the narthex—the assembly area—in front of the great portal, which was the grand entrance to the main body of the church itself, and was by all accounts the most elaborate and impressive sculptural ensemble that had been attempted in Europe since the days of Greece and Rome. But here the demolition squads of past centuries have done an even more thorough job—all that remains are the stubs of gigantic pillars, a double rank of them open to the sky and culminating in a tantalizing fragment of the massive portal that was once dominated by the central figure of Christ in Majesty.

At this point even the faintest echoes of the Middle Ages become inaudible for a while. There is no nave or chancel at all—instead a modern road crosses more or less where the water stoup would have been, leading to a car park that serves a handsome early nineteenth-century mansion which is now a hotel.

Beyond this point most of the old abbey is either lost altogether or buried beneath the modern town, though here and there a pillar or a fragment of carving throws up a reminder of what used to be here. Wandering the streets and alleys of Cluny can feel like exploring a giant skeleton. The sheer size of the medieval abbey comes as a constant surprise; for instance, when you stand by the ceremonial gateway looking eastwards, the trees far away on the edge of the town are actually where the church once extended. And beyond those trees runs the boundary wall, some of it still standing—huge slabs of sandstone that encircle the entire town, like a golden necklace strung with ancient towers.

One small part of the abbey church did manage to survive the depredations of those three citizens of Mâcon. It is surmounted by an octagonal tower in white limestone, the Clocher de l'Eau Bénite—Holy Water Belfry—that is visible for miles around, and naturally features on the covers of most of the local guidebooks. Anyone unfamiliar with the history of Cluny could be forgiven for assuming that this stately edifice represents the entire church, or at least most of it. In fact it is merely the southern arm of one transept—and Cluny boasted two transepts. But at least it provides a flavor of what the place must have been like. Its height is awesome—one hundred feet from floor to roof, and another fifty feet or so to the top of the tower—and as you gaze up it seems to rise forever. Multiply this transept arm by four, then add a nave that was two hundred and fifty feet in length, plus four aisles, plus a choir with its broad ambulatory and multiple radial chapels, not to mention the narthex—and suddenly the sheer immensity of this place, as well as the daring and skill of those who built it nearly a thousand years ago, becomes almost shockingly clear.

Pieces of the giant skeleton crop up all over the town. A spacious building that used to be the abbey's granary, with a magnificent barrel-vaulted roof, is now a small museum, the Musée du Farinier. Facing the entrance is a model of what the main portal and façade of the abbey church would have looked like. Next to this is a model of the interior, showing the eastern end, with the high altar, rounded ambulatory and apsidal chapels—and in case anyone should still be in doubt about the vastness of the church, tiny figures of monks have been placed here and there inside the model.

The gems of this museum are arranged at the far end of the room. There is a group of ten capitals, each one exquisitely carved on all four sides, and eight of which originally half encircled the choir of the abbey church; the other two served as supports to the apse beyond the choir at the eastern end. They are the earliest examples of figurative sculpture in Burgundy, and, despite their mutilation, it is astonishing how delicate and sophisticated they are; there is nothing whatever of the primitive about them, as if they had emerged fully fledged out of nowhere. Two of the capitals show figures representing the eight tones of the Gregorian chant for which Cluny was famous, and they are so skillfully sculptured that they appear to flutter and dance across the surface of the stone, accompanying you with the imaginary sound of singing as you walk round them. They are among the most precious remains of the former abbey, and it is one of the few happy accidents attending the place that they should have survived at all, having been rescued from the ransacking early in the nineteenth century by a certain Dr. Ochier who, as a boy, had known and loved the abbey before the wreckers moved in.

Dr. Ochier's name used to be given to what today is more prosaically termed the Musée d'Art et d'Archéologie. And here the search for Cluny becomes more evocative as well as more tantalizing. It is a museum of precious fragments painstakingly excavated over the recent decades—carved friezes, monumental capitals, geometrically decorated columns, sculpted monsters and human heads, fruits and flowers, lengths of tiled paving, every small example of which brings home just how much was irrevocably lost. There is the mythical figure of a mermaid, nearby a carved roundel of the Lamb of God three feet across, and at the far end of the room the most moving object of them all—a bare slab of pale marble, with an engraved border of ornamental foliage, which is almost certainly the surface of the high altar that was put in place for the formal consecration of the great abbey church by Pope Urban II in November 1095. The simplicity and delicacy of the piece comes as a surprise: that an institution so often defamed over the centuries for its opulence should have at its center of worship an object of such modesty is the most eloquent answer to its critics.

In the tenth, eleventh, and twelfth centuries Cluny was a phenomenon, but one that is particularly hard to comprehend in our more pragmatic and secular times. The very idea that a monastery, which by definition has isolated itself from the busy world, should become the capital of a veritable empire is a concept which requires some grasp of the condition of Christian Europe in the early Middle Ages, and of the temper and workings of the medieval mind—insofar as we can ever truly comprehend it.

In those distant days it was the monasteries that held a vital key to the shaping of a new Europe. They acted as colleges, patrons of art and architecture, moral guardians, benevolent landlords, founders of social services, centers of capital wealth, as well as being institutions of vast political influence on an international scale, with the ear of kings, emperors, and popes.

To a large extent their position of importance arose as a result of the prevailing chaos of the times. The empire forged by Charlemagne in the late eighth century broke apart not long after its creator's death in 814, due chiefly to the absence of any leader powerful enough to hold it together in the face of so many warring factions. As a result there followed a lengthy period of political anarchy throughout much of the continent. During the ninth and early tenth centuries marauders from three sides—north, east, and south—took full advantage of the fragility of western Europe. Magyars, Vikings, and Saracens descended in repeated waves of pillage and plunder. Nowhere was safe, and the Christian world was afraid.

There was another, deeper, fear, one that was fanned by the only spiritual teaching available, that of the church. This was the fear of Divine Punishment. In this destabilized world, where illiteracy was universal (except within some parts of the church), and ignorance of anything beyond the farm gate was almost total, it would have been small comfort to ordinary people to be told from the pulpit that all the horrors and deprivations of this life were no more than the result of their own sins. The early medieval church taught remorselessly that the human race lived under the stern judgment of God, and that his punishment was imminent. The end of the world was nigh, and everywhere you looked offered the first clear signs of it. Every flash of lightning, every eclipse, every flood or famine was a forewarning.

Because teaching was, in effect, a church monopoly, few people had access to any more rational and optimistic view of life. The truth was what they were told was true. The writings of the Greek philosophers, along with all other works of classical literature, were either unknown to the few who were capable of reading them—the literati—or were dismissed by the church as pagan heresy. It was several centuries before the new universities would begin to open students' eyes to Aristotelian logic, and Christian theologians (Thomas Aquinas in particular) would strive to refresh moribund Christian thought with welcome infusions of classical learning.

Meanwhile it was widely held, by lords and peasants alike, that humankind, if left to itself, was destined for hell. Only one institution was believed to possess the authority to intercede on its behalf on the Day of Judgment—and that was the monastery. Hence the sole hope of salvation, of remission of an individual's sins, lay with the prayers of the monks. Because they had abandoned the physical world in favor of the spiritual, only they had the ear of God. And the more fervent their prayers, the more inclined God might be to listen.

And so, in this frightened and unstable world the monasteries became the ark of salvation, and the monastic ideal acquired a spiritual accreditation that was unquestioned in every walk of human life. The peasant felt comforted by the distant tolling of the abbey bell, and by the knowledge that the devotions of the good monks were putting in a word for him and his family up above. As for the local lord, he could choose to pave his own path to heaven either by ending his days in a monastery, or alternatively by using his wealth to found or endow one.

Inevitably, then, the restoration of moral and social order in Europe became primarily the responsibility of the monasteries.

And this in turn required the monasteries to put their own house in order. By the tenth century many religious communities had slipped a considerable distance from the monastic disciplines set down in the sixth century by Benedict of Nursia, founder of the Benedictine order. Simony, the buying and selling of church offices and goods, was commonplace. Church lands were widely appropriated for personal gain. Illiterate local lords regularly appointed bishops and abbots for political or nepotistic reasons. The predecessors of Chaucer's Pardoner did a roaring trade exploiting people's credulity—salvation was up for sale. Monasteries themselves were poorly maintained. Many of the monks paid no more than lip service to their monastic vocation, eating and drinking to excess, attending church services when the hunting season permitted, and openly cohabiting with wives and mistresses.

The anarchic condition of Europe meant that the reform of monasteries inevitably acquired a political as well as moral significance. The rebirth of Europe depended upon it. And so, in answer to this need, there gradually emerged a small number of dedicated churchman determined to stamp out the prevailing abuses in monastic life, and to insist that the Rule of St. Benedict be observed at all times—to the very letter, and sometimes beyond. The dynamic of such a reform movement was a spirit of the most intense zeal and puritanical fervor, what one historian, Joan Evans, has described as "the ascetic ferocity of mediaeval religion." The driving force behind monastic reform was an iron determination to cleanse the Christian world of its impurities, and to establish a rule of life, a daily standard, which would be a model for all Christians to emulate, or at least to measure themselves against.

Regrettably, in accordance with church teaching, the most telling factor in this cleansing process was the conviction that one of these impurities from which the world needed to be cleansed was female sexual temptation. Medieval theologians had scarcely advanced beyond the book of Genesis as far as any understanding of human relationships between men and women was concerned. The church continued to hold a highly simplistic view of such things: there was Adam, and there was Eve, and the downfall of man was entirely Eve's fault. What was more, it was all about sex, and that was deemed to be Eve's doing, too. Adam had been seduced.

Hence the spectre of women's sexual power over men haunted the medieval church with a terrible passion, as any number of

sadistic stone carvings testify all too nakedly. The church had inherited from the desert fathers, and above all from St. Jerome, in the fourth century, the conviction that the female sex represented all the snares of the world, and that the only pure way to live one's life was to remain celibate. Except when they were needed for procreation purposes, women were safe only when they were in a nunnery and far away.

It remains one of the overwhelming contradictions of the Middle Ages that an ethos which was so dogmatic and doom-laden, so misogynist, so moralistic and disapproving of all the sensuous pleasures of day-to-day life, should yet have succeeded in creating so much that is the very opposite of those attitudes. What Cluny bequeathed to us is far from being the product of a hair-shirt culture—in a great many fields it is a legacy of serene beauty and sophistication that we still admire a thousand years later.

The answer to this apparent anomaly can only lie in what we see before us. The Cluniacs were among the most lavish and enlightened builders Europe has ever known, and the landscape of western Europe remains richly decorated with their achievements. They may have built for God, but the beneficiary has been humanity. In stone carving and wall painting, metalwork and book illumination, they were pioneers responsible for some of the most beautiful art of the Middle Ages. In music the Cluniac psalmody remains the finest example of Gregorian chant ever composed—it can hardly be an accident that the tunnel vaulting which Cluny's stonemasons perfected for their churches produces an acoustic that is ideally suited to the resonant chanting of a monastic choir. To listen to these psalms sung in one of the Romanesque churches of Burgundy raised by Cluniac masons is enough to dispel any thoughts of hellfire and damnation.

None of it is the art of doom—quite the reverse. Everything the Cluniacs produced, whether it was sculptures, frescoes, illuminated manuscripts, decorative arts, or liturgical music, rises triumphantly above the bigoted world in which it was created. Maybe there is a connection here—forbidden to create actual life, they poured their creativity into symbolic things. The art inspired by Cluny is grandiloquent and uplifting—it is the art of men who have seen the light, and are glorying in it. In their eyes richness and splendor spoke not of human vanity but of the glories of heaven. Nothing was too magnificent for God, so they set about honoring him with all the wealth and artifice the efforts of humankind could provide.

Yet it had all begun so very simply.

II

A Hunting Lodge in a
Secluded Valley

In the year 910 two men in their sixties were riding together along the valley of the River Grosne, flanked by wooded hills, a short distance from the town of Mâcon. One of the men was a monk by the name of Berno, a Burgundian nobleman who was abbot of the renowned monastery of Baume-les-Messieurs, a hard day's ride to the northeast. Berno had been summoned here by his riding companion, who was not only an aristocrat but among the most powerful figures in France, Duke William of Aquitaine. The area through which the two men were riding on that particular day was not actually part of William's duchy, but since his many titles included that of Count of Mâcon he was accordingly the owner of this valley as well as much of the surrounding region.

The duke's purpose in summoning Abbot Berno was a pious one, a determination to found a monastery on his own lands; and Berno, a churchman whom William deeply respected, was the man he had entrusted with the task of choosing the site. The duke's motives were mixed. He was a devout Christian. But he was also growing old and infirm. He was widowed, and his only son was dead. Furthermore, he had once committed a murder. In consequence, having no heir, and with the burden of sin on his shoulders, founding a monastery seemed the most desirable step to take before he died.

What William failed to foresee was that Berno, having by this time ridden over an extensive swathe of the duke's lands, would finally decide that this secluded river valley, protected by gentle forested hills, was the perfect place for the proposed monastery, and in particular the site of the modest building in front of them—which happened to be William's favorite hunting lodge. The duke was dismayed by his friend's choice but felt unable to go back on his word if the abbot insisted. Berno did insist, and he was not a man to mince his words: "Drive your hounds hence, and put monks in their place, because you know which will serve you better before God, the baying of hounds or the prayers of monks."

In fact these words were put into Berno's mouth by a fellow monk who was not even alive in 910—the eleventh-century chronicler Raoul Glaber. Nonetheless, their sentiments ring true to the emerging spirit of these times. In any event, the duke's own ambitions for his proposed monastery proved to be just as zealous as those of the abbot. It was important, he insisted, "that this benefaction may endure not only for a time, but may last for ever."

And so the lodge, or villa, of *Cluniacum*, as it had been known since Roman times, became the property of Abbot Berno, to do with it whatever he considered to be best. Precisely what the property consisted of is unclear. The Latin word *villa* had come to mean more than a single private dwelling, though still some way from the modern French *ville* or *village*. Our word "hamlet" probably comes closest. There are several documents of the ninth century which describe the property as being a small estate with a church, various other types of building, with fields, vineyards, orchards, woods, watercourses, and a number of resident families. In other words it was a settlement of some kind. The place seems once to have been owned by a member of Charlemagne's family. And by the late ninth century it was in the possession of Duke William's sister, a certain Ava. Then a document drawn up in the year 893 records that, having decided to become a nun, Ava, a "humble servant of Christ," left her villa of Cluny to her brother William, Duke of Aquitaine and Count of Auvergne."

Berno's choice of site was a shrewd one. Raoul Glaber wrote that "it was a valley shut off, far from all human contact." This, of course, was what had made it a natural sanctuary for deer, wild boar, and other game—hence Duke William's attachment to the place. But it was also a region relatively free from the interminable political struggles all around it; the centers of kingly or princely power in France were far away. Here was a quasi-neutral zone between the lands to the east of Mâcon and the River Saône, known as the County of Burgundy, which was part of the Holy Roman Empire ruled by the German king-emperors, and those lands to the west of the Saône which formed part of the Duchy of Burgundy, owing allegiance to France.

More important still, it was a region whose geographical position between two major rivers, the Saône to the east and the Loire to the west, gave it a certain protection from the plundering of invaders. Several of the existing monasteries in Burgundy had been settled within the previous century by monks fleeing the Vikings—the "Norman fury"—in the north, while other areas had been repeatedly desolated by Magyar horsemen swooping in from the east, or by Saracens launching raids from Islamic territories in Spain, Sicily, and North Africa.

By the time Duke William and Abbot Berno agreed to found their new monastery here some of these dangers had already started to recede. The Norman threat effectively ended the following year, 911. A peace treaty was signed, the Normans settled down, accepted

Christianity, French law and language, and Normandy became a duchy ruled by a remarkable dynasty—which in the century to come was to produce William the Conqueror. Europe was moving further from the so-called Dark Ages.

Duke William did not simply hand over the property to Berno as an act of piety and leave him to it. He drew up a carefully worded foundation charter for the new monastery and signed it in his home city of Bourges on September 11, 910; it remains one of the seminal documents in church history, characterized by its foresight and by a touching humility and generosity of spirit.

> I will provide at my expense for men living together under monastic vows, with this hope and faith, that if I cannot myself despise all the things of this world, at least by sustaining those who do despise the world, those whom I believe to be righteous in the eyes of God, I may myself receive the rewards of righteousness.... Our foundation shall serve forever as a refuge for those who, having renounced the world as poor men, bring nothing with them but their good will, and we desire that our superfluity shall become their abundance.

The most telling component of William's charter, one that was to have a far-reaching effect on Cluny's future as well as on the future of monasticism in general, was the duke's insistence that the new monastery be totally exempt from any ecclesiastical or lay authority or interference, including interference by the founder himself or his family. Instead, Cluny was to be placed within the sole authority of the papacy in Rome, under the protection of St. Peter and St. Paul. (The symbols of the two saints, the keys of St. Peter and the sword of St. Paul, were to become the abbey's coat of arms.)

This stipulation was a brave one because it was guaranteed to cause trouble; only one of the most powerful aristocrats of the day could have got away with it. At a stroke it excluded local bishops, feudal lords, and church and lay authorities generally, from having any say whatsoever in the running of the place, or in the appointment of the abbot and other senior monks. Abbot Berno was to be fully in charge of the monks and of the monastery's property, the duke insisted. Then after Berno's death, "the same monks should have the power and permission to elect as abbot and rector whomever they prefer of their order." (In practice it seems generally to have become the privilege of the incumbent abbot to nominate his successor, probably after consultation with his fellow monks.)

The immediate significance of Duke William's charter was to forestall any of the customary practices of simony, nepotism, and self-advantage that the local church and secular authorities would certainly otherwise have imposed—a new and well-endowed religious house was something to be bled. However, by creating a *cordon sanitaire* round the new foundation, Cluny inevitably, and for much of its history, became the object of local jealousies, and would always attract local enemies ready to stamp on it if they could.

The long-term effect of the charter was vastly to increase the authority of Cluny itself as its empire began to expand beyond anything the duke or Abbot Berno could possibly have imagined. Indirectly, too, it was to boost the influence and power of the papacy once Cluny became the Vatican's most trusted champion and ambassador.

Little is known about Cluny itself in these very early years. And we hear no more from Duke William, who died in 918. Meanwhile, Berno set about creating the new religious community. He brought about twelve monks from Baume-les-Messieurs, where he still remained abbot, most likely installing them in the building that had been William's hunting lodge. The church mentioned in the ninth-century documents was probably no more than a simple private chapel made of wood, of which there was a plentiful local supply. Berno soon began the construction of a larger church (labeled by historians as Cluny I), probably also of wood, a short distance to the north of the villa. This new church was consecrated in the year 916 or 917, and proved to be inadequate within a single generation, which suggests that by the time Abbot Berno died in 926 or 927 the number of resident monks must have risen considerably, all of them presumably supported by Duke William's estate.

In accordance with the duke's charter, Berno, as he approached death, exercised his privilege in appointing his successor. The second abbot of Cluny was a man in his forties by the name of Odo, and we know quite a lot about him because a contemporary and admirer by the name of John of Salerno wrote a glowing biography. Even setting aside John's somewhat uncritical eulogies, Odo emerges as the first of a string of remarkable abbots which Cluny was fortunate to possess over the following two centuries. Like his predecessor, Odo was an aristocrat. He had been brought up in Duke William's court before becoming a monk at the abbey of St. Martin at Tours, and subsequently at Baume-les-Messieurs, where he came to the notice of Abbot Berno.

John of Salerno describes him as saintly—naturally—but more specifically as a warm and charming man whose fellow monks used to refer to as *fossor*, the "digger," on account of his eyes being steadfastly downcast at all times. He was also a poet and musician. This latter attribute is particularly relevant in view of the sophisticated musical tradition that was soon to grow up at Cluny—

and it is reasonable to suppose that it was Odo who established this tradition during the fifteen years of his abbacy.

As important as his musical gifts and his saintliness were Odo's worldly talents. Berno's young Cluny had been poor in the extreme. All monasteries needed bequests and an income from land in order to survive, and once Duke William had died Cluny had little of either. In fact Berno had been compelled to divert funds from another monastery, Gigny, of which he was also the abbot.

There can be no doubt that for Odo, as for Berno, aristocratic connections helped to overcome hardship—indeed, Cluny would never have become what it was without them. Both men were Burgundian noblemen. Odo also seems to have had notable powers of persuasion. As a result, the combination of the personal influence he wielded and Cluny's growing reputation for moral probity soon began to attract gifts of land, which supported the monastery. At times these gifts also included other abbeys within Burgundy considered to be too lax in discipline and in need of the reforming guidance of Cluny's highly esteemed abbot. Both in finance and in reputation Cluny was beginning to become a small power in the land.

The ability of the young monastery to attract so much powerful support was to a great extent a product of the new feudal society. Feudalism—that finely adjusted ladder of legal obligations running from top to bottom of European society—emerged in response to the failure of established authorities to deal with the foreign invasions that had repeatedly savaged the continent of Europe since the eighth century. The primary need everywhere was protection, and a social system grew up in order to provide it. The lynchpin was the local lord, the count, to whom everyone on his lands owed allegiance as his vassal. He effectively owned them, and in return undertook to protect them. His castle was his fortress, paid for by the taxes he extracted. But the local lord would in turn be the vassal of some overlord to whom he, too, had legal obligations. He could be required at his own expense to contribute foot soldiers and, above all, mounted knights in the event of invasion or rebellion. In a feudal society everyone had an allegiance to somebody else, and the result was a widespread social regrouping which played an enormous part in the resurgence of Europe.

Feudalism first emerged as a social system in Europe in the Frankish kingdom as early as the eighth century. Then, with Frankish conquests in Italy, Germany, Spain, and elsewhere, the system spread throughout much of the continent, eventually reaching England with the Norman Conquest of 1066. Alongside the secular world the medieval church also became largely feudalized—by mutual benefit to those concerned; in return for the required homage and obligations of service, noblemen would liberally grant investitures on grateful bishops and abbots, along with the lucrative material benefits which came with high ecclesiastical office.

The effect of this new social order on Cluny, and on monasticism in general, was dramatic. The new class of noblemen, elevated and enriched by the feudal system, were military men, knights whose ambition in the course of time would include the dogmatic determination to drive foreign powers, in particular Muslims, from Christian lands. Accordingly, the blessing of Christ's servants here on earth was essential to their cause. As a result, huge sums of money began to be invested in the building of churches, often accompanied by equally lavish bequests and gifts of land and property. And the reward for such investments was the most sought-after benefit of all—salvation. Feudal lords bought their seats in heaven, and in exchange the monasteries became seats of power on earth.

But in one respect, as mentioned, Cluny was different. While other monasteries were subject to the usual feudal bonds, Duke William's charter specifically freed Cluny from all outside authority except the Vatican. No local lord, however powerful he might be, and however generous his benefaction, could exert any influence on the abbey whatsoever. At the same time, although Cluny was independent of all feudal obligations outside the abbey, within its walls its own system of authority was rigidly adhered to. All monks were bound in obedience to their abbot just as strictly as a serf working in the fields was bound in vassalage to his feudal lord. The abbot was a feudal lord in his own right. Yet he too had a master to answer to, no less an eminence than the pope himself.

This was why, in the year 931, four years after becoming abbot, Odo traveled to Rome specifically in order to obtain from Pope John XI confirmation of Cluny's special status. The fact that he undertook such a journey—an arduous one on horseback with any number of attendant dangers—is proof of the fragility of Cluny's independence at the time, and of the persistent threat to it posed by local interests and jealousies in Burgundy. Only the word of the pope could safeguard that independence. Odo obtained it—the first of many such confirmations of Cluny's special privilege that successive popes were to offer. Undoubtedly mutual self-interest played its part. The papacy may have been able to claim an unassailable spiritual authority as head of the church, yet in political and temporal terms it remained vulnerably weak. Compared to the power and influence wielded by the Holy Roman emperors, the popes' actual authority was limited, and all too frequently challenged or brushed aside. Hence nothing could have been more welcome to a weak papacy than a new rising power within the church which had been placed specifically under its protection. On the other hand the abbots of Cluny felt it equally welcome to be able to use the legal shield of the Vatican as a protection against powerful local pressures in Burgundy.

Abbot Odo was a man of drive and no mean courage. He shared his predecessor's reforming zeal, and his most ardent ambition was to enforce the Rule of St. Benedict in those monasteries that were beginning to come under the authority of Cluny. Benedict of Nursia had composed his Rule in the sixth century for the benefit of the monastery he founded at Monte Cassino, in Italy south of Rome. Had it been a rigid and punitive document, Odo might well not have succeeded in imposing it. As it was, the strength of the Rule lay in its balance, gentleness, and humanity. While it demanded complete obedience, personal poverty, and chastity to assure communal stability, there was nothing unnecessarily authoritarian about it. Benedict's aim had been to offer a succinct and essentially humane directory for the government and well-being of a monastery, set down in a spirit of moderation, and with a frank allowance for human weakness and failure. Monks were to be allowed good food and wine, clothes that were suited to the climate and the seasons, and an opportunity to use a number of manual or creative skills. Each day's goal was to achieve a balance of prayer, work, and study, four or five hours being recommended for each.

Nonetheless, we know from Odo's biographer, John of Salerno, that his interventions were not always well received. One visit was to a monastery particularly close to his heart. Several days' ride northwest of Cluny along the River Loire lay the abbey of St. Benoît, so named because it claimed to possess the body of St. Benedict himself, allegedly taken there by monks in the seventh century following the destruction of Benedict's original monastery at Monte Cassino. Since that time St. Benoît had grown wealthy as a result of the prodigious number of miracles and cures attributed to the saint's relics, and the monks were in no mood to accept the stringent disciplines being proposed by their unwanted visitor. Accordingly they greeted Odo and his entourage with a violent show of arms, and it took all the abbot's powers of diplomacy to wear down their hostility. John of Salerno, though not actually present at the scene, quotes Odo's words to the assembled monks once he had finally gained entry: "I come peacefully, to hurt no one, injure no one, only that I may convert those who are not living according to the Rule."

A few years later, by now over sixty, Odo undertook a far more arduous journey, all the way to Monte Cassino itself, now rebuilt, in order to pay his respects to Benedict's foundation and to establish cordial relations with its abbot. For a Christian, and especially a

Benedictine monk, there were few places quite as holy—and accessible— as Monte Cassino at this time. Jerusalem was part of the Islamic world. Rome had yet to acquire the grandeur and the mystique that were to adorn it in the centuries to come. Santiago de Compostela, in northwest Spain, and its shrine of the apostle St. James, was all but inaccessible since much of the journey was through Muslim lands. And Monte Cassino, naturally, held a special appeal for all Benedictines as the seat of their founder and the birthplace of their Rule.

The wide dissemination of St. Benedict's Rule is largely due to Charlemagne and the scholars of his court, men with a reverence for antique knowledge and the desire to find and copy the original texts of the early church. It is recorded that early in the ninth century the emperor obtained from Monte Cassino a copy of the original version of the Rule. Charlemagne's teacher and adviser was the renowned English scholar Alcuin, and it was Alcuin who is believed to have urged the emperor to instigate the task of imposing the Rule on a number of lapsed monasteries within his empire. So began a reforming movement within the Benedictine world which was later carried on by Charlemagne's son, Louis the Pious, and subsequently—and triumphantly—by Cluny itself.

Hence the abbots of Cluny were proud to see themselves, spiritually at least, as heirs of the great Emperor Charlemagne and his scholarly court. Yet it was this very inheritance that was to draw Odo's successors, whether willingly or unwillingly, into one political battlefield after another as uneasy peacemakers in the most dramatic conflict of the century to come, that titanic struggle for the leadership of Christianity between the popes in Rome and the Holy Roman emperors in Germany.

III.

The Stonemasons from Italy

 Odo died just two years after returning from Monte Cassino, in 942. He was sixty-three. Perhaps because so commanding a figure at the helm had passed from the scene there followed what seems like a period of calm in the fortunes of Cluny. Odo's successor for the next twenty years has left only a small mark on the history of the place. He was a monk by the name of Aymard, and little is known about him beyond a reputation for being an innocent and simple soul, and the fact that for the last several years of his abbacy he was blind.

But before his sight completely left him Aymard chose in 954 as his coadjutor abbot and eventual successor a man who was to make a massive impact on the future of the abbey. This was Mayeul or, in the Latin version used in contemporary records, Maiolus. In any case French would not have been the new abbot's natural tongue. Mayeul was a Provençal, and therefore would have been brought up to speak that derivative of Latin in southern France known to us as *langue d'oc*, the language of the troubadours which is akin to modern Catalan and is still spoken in remoter areas of the south. However, Mayeul, like his predecessors at Cluny, was a nobleman, and to judge by some remarkable family connections he must certainly have been multilingual. One of his friends was none other than the king of France. Another was an even bigger name, the Holy Roman emperor, Otto II. The latter was so impressed by his Cluniac friend that he proposed him as pope, an elevation which Mayeul graciously (and perhaps wisely) declined, though on several occasions he performed the delicate role of mediator in disputes between emperor and pope.

Like all the great abbots of Cluny, Mayeul was a man of immense charisma. He is described as handsome, warm, and charming, as well as being an excellent administrator. He was also a scholar, a man highly educated and—a rarity in the monastic world at that time—a former student of the classics before becoming a monk. Added to these accomplishments was a certain glamour, heightened no doubt by the fact that while he was abbot he was once kidnapped by Saracens in his native Provence, only to be expensively ransomed by his distinguished family.

This was the man who in the year 963 was led to the abbot's throne after the death of Aymard. The abbey church in which this ceremony took place, Abbot Berno's Cluny I, had long since become too small for the community. Accordingly, it was already in the process of being enlarged and rebuilt, eventually to become what today we refer to as Cluny II. This new church was not actually completed until well into the following century, long after Mayeul's death; however, basic building works had begun under his supervision as early as 955, or even before, which clearly suggests that Mayeul was already *de facto* abbot for—at the least—the long period of Aymard's blindness.

The dedication of the new church took place in 981, but it was only after this date that full-scale construction work was finally set in motion.

The design of Cluny II remains a milestone in the history of church architecture. Many of its features were soon to become commonplace, yet they were daring and original at the time. These included an apse, the area beyond the choir and the high altar, which was made up of three separate chapels, each radiating outwards in the manner of a cloverleaf. There was also a spacious covered entrance to the church, the narthex, large enough to accommodate the entire Sunday procession. And above the narthex rose twin bell towers, rectangular in shape. An even taller tower rose above the crossing, the area in a crucifix-shaped church where nave and transept intersect. The nave itself was long and narrow, its roof vaulted in the form of a long tunnel, like an inverted pipe. This design of a tunnel vault became the prototype for a great number of churches soon to be built under the auspices of Cluny, especially those in the towns and villages of southern Burgundy. It was favored above other forms of vaulting, so later reports make clear, because its hollow acoustics perfectly suited the ritual chanting of plainsong which was such a key component of Cluniac services.

The building of Cluny II was the first major contribution Mayeul was to make to the expansion of the abbey. Sadly, for all its innovative features, the church enjoyed a relatively brief life, a victim of Cluny's expansion and worldly success; it was pulled down and replaced by the colossal structure labeled Cluny III (which is the present-day ruin) less than a century later. But we have a fairly clear picture of what Cluny II would have looked like, partly from graphic reconstructions drawn by the architectural scholar Kenneth John Conant in the mid-twentieth century, but also from a number of surviving parish churches in Burgundy which are known to have been based on its design—children of Cluny II, so to speak.

It is here that Mayeul's second, even larger, contribution to the story of Cluny comes into play. In the year 987 he used his prestige as abbot, and no doubt his aristocratic connections, to persuade one of the most remarkable men of his day to come to Cluny. This was an Italian nobleman whose relatives included just about every living grandee in Europe, and his godmother was the wife of the Holy Roman emperor. It would have been hard to be better connected. This paragon was William (or Guglielmo) of Volpiano, and he was neither a prince nor a duke, but a young monk—at the abbey of San Michele de Locedia, in the Piedmont region of northern Italy.

William of Volpiano shared with the abbots of Cluny a determination to reform monasteries whose way of life had lapsed. Furthermore, and of particular significance in the context of Cluny, he was also a highly gifted designer. He was in effect (to use a modern term) an architect. And it was in this capacity that this aristocratic monk occupies a special niche in history, because it was he more than anyone who was responsible for establishing the first truly international style of church architecture in Europe. He was the father of the Romanesque—or, more accurately, its godfather.

The term "Romanesque" describes, broadly speaking, a style of building which is derived from what was known of Ancient Roman architecture. When applied to early medieval churches it is identified by such features as rounded arches and windows, simple classical columns with carved capitals, and usually a rounded apse beyond the altar at the eastern end. It became the predominant form of church architecture for over two hundred years until the evolution of the Gothic style late in the twelfth century. But even though Romanesque architecture embraces a broad variety of buildings, from vast cathedrals to thousands of village churches right across Europe, it was actually born in monasteries; and if not exactly born in Burgundy, then it first grew and flourished there under the aegis of Cluny. To this day many of the towns and villages in the region possess Romanesque parish churches in a distinctive Burgundian style, which owes it origin to the talents of William of Volpiano and to the power and initiative of a succession of abbots of Cluny.

It is quite likely that Abbot Mayeul's purpose in luring William to Burgundy was initially to carry out the reform of religious houses, in particular the historic monastery of St. Bénigne in Dijon (where William became abbot), and ultimately to do the same with a host of other morally lapsed monastic houses in the Duchy of Burgundy and beyond, many of which had by now come under Cluny's ever-widening umbrella.

This process of reform meant not simply putting these religious houses back in order by imposing the Rule of St. Benedict; it also meant *building*. And building on a vast scale. Such an ambition demanded not only funds, which were soon made available, but it also required a workforce capable of doing the job. Both William and Abbot Mayeul knew that no master masons and stonecarvers of sufficient skill existed within the duchy at that time. Only one region of Europe possessed such craftsmen, and that, as it happened, was where William's noble family held sway: Lombardy. There, in northern Italy, existed a body of architectural craftsmen of precisely the kind Mayeul and William needed.

It remains something of a mystery why this should have been so given the state of political anarchy that had long prevailed in Lombardy. Its capital city, Milan, had enjoyed success and prosperity in Roman times, and it has been suggested that building skills may have survived even the darkest years after Rome's fall. A tradition of architectural excellence most likely existed in Lombardy at least as early as the seventh century, since a royal charter at that time made reference to special privileges awarded to skilled master masons and carvers. They were referred to as *magistri comacini*. Clearly these *magistri* were highly respected; the most likely interpretation of *comacini* is that they flourished in the area around Lake Como. Then, in the eighth century, Lombardy was conquered by the Franks under Charlemagne, and in the ensuing religious revival the next hundred years witnessed a flowering of church architecture throughout the region, much of it being quite distinct in style and very evidently the work of this same guild of *magistri comacini*.

Here was one of the cradles of the Romanesque style of church building. And these were the very Lombard craftsmen whom William of Volpiano decided to bring to Burgundy in order to carry out the work Abbot Mayeul required. We do not know how many of them crossed the Alps, but they must have been quite numerous considering the number of monasteries, priories, and parish churches within a short radius of Cluny that were built in what has become known as the First Romanesque style. They all bear the unmistakable hallmarks of the Lombards—tall slender bell towers, decorative blind arches set into the walls, saw-edged molding round the roofline of the apse—so much so that *Lombardus* soon became the local generic term for a mason. We know that they operated within a system of itinerant workshops, part of an extended mobile community that would have included wives, families, and servants. These people were essentially nomadic; if they retained a home base in their native Lombardy it must have been a fairly tenuous one, and many of them probably never set foot in Italy all their lives. They stayed in one place only until a job was done, which might be several decades, after which they moved on, traveling from town to town, country to country, plying their skills as work became available. The buildings they left behind mark out their wanderings over a period of well over a hundred years. Lombard work can be traced to Germany (in particular the cathedrals of Mainz, consecrated in 1009, and Speyer, 1061), as far north as Sweden (the cathedral of Lund, 1145), as far east as Dalmatia and Hungary, and as far west as Catalonia, where the monasteries round the slopes of Mont Canigou, such as St. Martin du Canigou and Serrabonne, carry the clear signature of the Lombards.

In the course of their travels they would have absorbed local skills and traditions, and certainly they would have trained local talent wherever they went, as a result of which Cluny itself soon came to possess its own stonemason's yard with its own builders and carvers who within a hundred years were to become the most gifted sculptors in Europe.

But that is looking further ahead. Among the special skills which these early craftsmen brought with them from Lombardy was that of stone vaulting—and this was to prove particularly valuable to Cluny at a time when ever-increasing gifts of land and property were necessitating the building of numerous new churches in the region. (The astonishing number of 630 such gifts is recorded between the foundation of Cluny in 910 and the year 980.) Stone vaulting, replacing the highly flammable wooden roofs of pre-Romanesque church buildings, allowed the creation of spacious interiors, the roof supported by massive walls and solid columns. The Lombards also developed a new kind of wall construction which was both decorative and extremely practical—small stones being split into bricklike shapes laid diagonally in high-quality mortar to form rhythmical patterns, sometimes varied by irregular stones or rounded river pebbles.

For all their ambitious undertakings the Lombards' building methods remained rudimentary and traditional. Measuring tools consisted simply of knotted ropes and cords; a rope would bear a knot every twelve inches, marking out what was a Roman foot (which in itself suggests just how long such a system had been employed). As for matters of design, symbolism ruled in everything they did; nothing was without a hidden sacred meaning, developed by philosophers and theologians over many centuries. The dimensions of an entire church were determined by sacred geometry. The number Seven was especially holy; it symbolized the seven days of creation, and was the sum of Three, representing the Holy Trinity, and Four, which stood for the earth. A church would have seven altars, and its apse seven blind arches; candelabra would be seven-branched; columns would be set precisely seven feet apart. Gregorian chant consisted of eight tones, and some towers were built as octagons, because Eight was the number of the *new* creation—the "eighth day," when the divine order was completed. There was even a practice of making a church nave 153 feet wide, this being believed to be the number of fish caught by St. Peter in the Miraculous Draft of Fishes. Symbolism was of importance because it was the way the medieval mind worked. The physical world was perceived to be a mere echo of the celestial, and therefore needed to be defined in terms that related to that celestial world.

But measuring by numbers also had its practical application—it offered an ideal discipline for those engaged in any building operation. It was appropriate and efficient and a working method that everyone could understand. After all, people might not be able to read, but they could count.

The character of southern Burgundy today is to a considerable extent the creation of these Lombard craftsmen. The churches they built, with their tall distinctive towers, still dominate the landscape, particularly in the area around Mâcon—the Mâconnais region.

Some twenty miles northeast of Cluny lies the small town of Tournus. And here on the banks of the River Saône rises the Lombard church par excellence—the abbey church of St. Philibert. From the outside it has something of the look of a fortress—and as well it might. During the eighth century Saracen invaders plundered the first monastery here. A hundred years later a community of monks at Noirmoutier, on the Atlantic coast, was driven out by Viking pirates and after a period of wandering settled in 875 at Tournus, bringing with them the relics of their patron saint, St. Philibert. In 937 Magyars—Hungarian marauders—partly destroyed their monastery along with much of the rest of Burgundy, completing the job when they returned eighteen years later. Then in 1006 the rebuilt church was gutted by a fire which killed several monks, only the crypt being spared. Finally, some sort of peace returned, and in 1019 the structure that essentially comprises the present church was consecrated, the finishing touches being added early in the twelfth century.

To this day St. Philibert is one of the most strikingly beautiful buildings in France. It is Lombard work at its most triumphant. The great flank of the church is a testimony not just to the Lombards' building prowess but to the way they could combine those rugged skills with a gift for the most delicate ornamentation in stone—motifs that we see repeated in church after church in the Mâconnais. What could otherwise have been a bare cliff of stone is made subtle, almost soft like embroidery. Vertical bands of blind arches are set into the wall, and these are accompanied by a tracery of saw-edged moldings and strips of zigzag stonework, all of which combine to make the wall itself appear multilayered instead of flat, light instead of heavy, almost transparent. Simply as a wall, it is a masterpiece.

The interior of St. Philibert is quite the reverse. Instead of trying to appear light, everything is made massive: huge, rose-colored pillars rise like trees from floor to barrel-vaulted ceiling, while at the western end a two-story narthex supports an upper chapel of elemental purity. Architecture can get no simpler than this, nor any grander. Tournus is a place that makes us conscious of a truism that is peculiarly moving: the absolute stillness of stone.

The monks of Tournus, the heirs of those wanderers who fled the Viking pirates, now began to expand their activities to embrace several of the smaller communities nearby. They commissioned Lombard masons to build a number of parish churches which, like their own abbey, would reflect the new spirit and religious fervor that followed the uneventful passing of the first Millennium—in spite of apocalyptic fears.

Nothing in church architecture expresses this reborn confidence more eloquently than the bell tower. The Lombard masons were particularly skilled at towers, having brought the tradition with them from northern Italy. Now in southern Burgundy the towers became a feature greatly in demand. In this new era of peace and self-confidence a church tower became the dominant feature of the landscape (as indeed it still is in rural areas of Burgundy and much of Europe). It was visible for miles around, soaring above the mean dwellings of a small town or village, and

sending its peals ringing far out over the forests and water meadows. A tower was a symbol of God's authority, his triumphant rule here on earth. It was also a promise, a finger pointing proudly to heaven.

The tower of St. Philibert at Tournus is one of the glories of early Romanesque architecture. Just a few miles downriver is a smaller version of it in the village of Farges, believed to have been built by the same Lombard masons, just like the even more beautiful church in the village of Uchizy, just half a mile away.

And some fifteen miles to the west, across this damp wooded landscape, lies the village of Chapaize. It is hardly bigger today than it would have been when the monks of Cluny founded a priory here in the tenth century, and even now the abbey church of St. Martin seems rather grandly out of scale with its modest surroundings. One glance at the lofty tower decorated with blind arches tells us who built it. The Lombards brought their well-tried skills here in the service of Cluny around the year 1000. The interior of Chapaize is a pure echo of Tournus, though with an added touch of elegance which comes as a surprise: each of its huge pillars flanking the nave has been given a simple V-shaped carving on all four sides, so breaking up the severe geometry of the place. Here once again these masons working for Cluny demonstrated what it takes to create a masterpiece—pure and beautiful, without elaborate artifice or showmanship, as though it came naturally, bred in the bone.

IV.

A White Mantle of Churches

Mayeul was abbot of Cluny for thirty-one years, and by the time he died, in 994, the abbey had come to support more than a hundred monks and was the heart of a monastic empire that extended far beyond its walls. Yet it was an empire under repeated threat. Political stability in Europe was fragile, to say the least, and there was constant fear of bloodshed, due to feuds among the local nobility as well continuing threats from foreign invaders. Twice in previous decades the abbey of Tournus had been attacked by the Magyars; and in the year of Mayeul's death the monastery of Monte Cassino, with which Cluny enjoyed close ties, had once again been sacked, this time by Saracens advancing north from their territory in Sicily.

Looming ever closer was a catastrophe that was even more grave, at least if the teachings of the church were to be believed. This was the day of fire and brimstone, the final reckoning for which the Christian world had been preparing itself for centuries: the Millennium—the one thousandth anniversary of the birth of Our Lord.

According to ecclesiastical orthodoxy the year 1000 was supposed to be the defining moment in the story of humankind. Unfortunately there has never been a solid body of agreement among historians or churchmen as to what the Millennium really meant to ordinary Christians at the time, if indeed it meant anything at all. How many people are likely to have been even aware of it, let alone grasped what it was supposed to mean? There was no disseminated information of any kind except from preachers. There was no forum of debate, no climate of questioning or skepticism. There were no reliable calendars. There was not even any agreement among church scholars as to the precise number of years that had elapsed since the birth of Christ, because for much of that time no one had thought to count. And if it was a question of referring to the authority of the Bible for any useful answers, few people could read it anyway.

So, what did people really imagine was going to happen at the first Millennium? And what in fact did happen when the dreaded moment finally arrived? In particular, what was its effect on Cluny?

The last of these questions is the only one that can be answered with any degree of confidence, because one of Cluny's monks has left us a brief but graphic account of what actually took place—the chronicler Raoul Glaber, who died around the year 1050. His five volumes of *Historiae* were dedicated to Abbot Odilo, who had succeeded to the abbacy after the death of Mayeul. Glaber's point of departure was the biblical source of the whole Millennium legend, the Revelation of John the Divine (otherwise known as the Apocalypse), chapters 20 to 22. Here are the appropriate passages taken from the lyrical translation of the King James Bible:

> And I saw an angel come down from heaven, having the key of the bottomless pit and a great chain in his hand. And he laid hold on the dragon, that old serpent, which is the Devil, and Satan, and bound him a thousand years, And cast him into the bottomless pit, and shut him up, and set a seal upon him, that

he should deceive the nations no more, till the thousand years be fulfilled: and after that he must be loosed a little season. . . .

And when the thousand years are expired, Satan shall be loosed out of his prison. And shall go out to deceive the nations which are in the four quarters of the earth. . . .

And I saw a new heaven and a new earth: for the first heaven and the first earth were passed away; and there was no more sea. And I John saw the holy city, new Jerusalem, coming down from God out of heaven, prepared as a bride adorned for her husband. . . . And he that sat upon the throne said, Behold, I make all things new. . . . I Jesus have sent mine angel to testify unto you these things in the churches. I am the root and the offspring of David, and the bright and morning star.

What is intriguing about these passages, which are the climax of John's vision of the new order of things, is that they are not actually about punishment, as one might have supposed. It is true that Satan is about to run riot, but only for "a little season," after which we are promised the "new Jerusalem," the eternal city of God, coming down from heaven as radiant as "a bride adorned for her husband." It would appear that too much emphasis has generally been laid by church fathers on the punitive aspects of John's prophesy, and too little on the strong message of hope that follows it.

And this makes Raoul Glaber's account of events at that time so pertinent and revealing. "A little after the year one thousand," he writes, "it came about that the churches were rebuilt throughout the known world. . . . One would have said that the world itself was casting aside its old age and clothing itself anew in a white mantle of churches. . . . A veritable contest drove each Christian community to build a more sumptuous church than its neighbors. . . . Even the little churches in the villages were reconstructed by the faithful more beautiful than before."

"A white mantle of churches" evokes a serene picture of a land dotted with pale sandstone buildings with tall bell towers and elegant carved portals—in fact remarkably like the rich landscape of Burgundy as it has survived in many places to this day. Glaber would have been thinking of William of Volpiano's rebuilt abbey of St. Bénigne in Dijon where he had spent his earlier years, and in particular Abbot Mayeul's new abbey church at Cluny (Cluny II) which he may well have witnessed being built. He would also have been thinking of the innumerable priories, convents, and parish churches that were springing up all over the Duchy of Burgundy during these early years of the eleventh century.

A thousand years later, the French *département* of Saône-et-Loire, to which Cluny belongs, still possesses almost 250 Romanesque churches of that early period that have survived either completely or at least substantially. While not every one of these churches owes its existence directly to Cluny, the abbey has left its indelible mark on virtually every town and village in southern Burgundy, and it is impossible to travel through this region and not be conscious of Cluny's watchful presence.

The best way to appreciate Raoul Glaber's "white mantle of churches" today is from a high hill. The village of Mont-St.-Vincent stands on a ridge two thousand feet above sea level and some fifteen miles to the northwest of Cluny. Far below, clusters of villages are separated from each other by a latticework of fields dotted with white Charolais cattle. Outlying farm buildings are spread out like wings, often surmounted by towers with roofs like witches' hats, serving as dovecots, the *pigeonniers*. In the village of Mont-St.-Vincent itself a narrow lane meanders between houses that look permanently silent in slumber, until at the end of the village the lane abruptly opens up in front of a rugged hulk of a church. The carved tympanum over the main door is in a battered state, but a familiar signature of Cluny is recognizable—the hieratic figure of Christ in Majesty set between the abbey's two patron saints, St. Peter and St. Paul.

This was once a Cluniac priory, founded in the eleventh century and of which, as so often, only the church survives. The interior, with its barrel-vaulted roof in the manner of Tournus, has that air of noble gloom which these early Romanesque churches in Burgundy so often possess.

Another narrow lane fringed with a sunburst of wildflowers leads to the edge of the ridge. And here, suddenly, is a reminder that medieval priories were not simply places of quiet worship for those in retreat—they were also fortresses. Stretches of a cyclopean wall line the ridge, each block of stone at least three feet in length and deftly slotted into those around it. Mont St. Vincent was a fortified mountain, to ward off marauders from nearby and afar.

Beyond, and far below, spreads the Burgundy Raoul Glaber might still recognize today. In the distance flows the long thread of the River Saône with the tall Lombard tower of Tournus directly to the east, and the diocesan capital of Mâcon a few miles downstream. A little to the southeast, and somewhat closer, is one of those jewels that would have been set into Glaber's "white mantle"—the secluded priory of Blanot, which was one of Cluny's oldest possessions. The village of Blanot is set beside a stream lined with willows and alders heavy with mistletoe, its banks carpeted with cowslips and bluebells in the spring. And in the middle of the village stands the former priory church that Glaber would have known, and may even have witnessed being built. It has all the familiar hallmarks of Lombard craftsmanship: blind arches, decorative patterns of stone tracery, a handsome bell tower—in this case with a curious overhanging roof like a hat several sizes too large. Altogether Blanot is the epitome of rural peace, a place where one can linger, wander, and lose any sense of time.

Further to the southeast rises the distant tower of Cluny itself, and not far, along the gentle valley of the Grosne, lies Mazille—a solid fortified village on a hill, accompanied by yet another magnificent Lombard church, St. Blaise. It is set well outside the village, dramatically isolated in the valley below among meadows golden with cowslips. If these early monks yearned for a paradise on earth, then maybe they sensed they had created it here.

All in all, Raoul Glaber's account of these postmillennial years is quite the opposite of what one might have expected from early medieval church teaching. Far from being an unrelenting cry of memento mori, his words sound a chord of universal relief and optimism. What they suggest is that a great fear had been lifted. The world had not been consumed by fire, and humankind had not been consigned to everlasting torment. There was a future. People could live and flourish. Now was the time to celebrate, to worship, and of course to build. And with this vast program of church building under way it was the abbey of Cluny, as Glaber makes quite clear, that was preparing itself for that New Jerusalem, the spiritual world to come here on this earth as predicted by John in the book of Revelation, and which was the ultimate hope of all the faithful.

It is not easy for us today to understand the influence of the book of Revelation on the medieval mind. Without question its importance in medieval art is enormous. There is hardly an illuminated manuscript or Romanesque church in the whole of

Europe that does not contain some lurid image inspired by John's vision of divine retribution—fantastic beasts, seven-headed dragons, gruesome scenes of punishment, demonic orgies, images of female lust. Medieval artists and the churchmen who commissioned them reveled in this nightmarish imagery. Yet there is a persistent anomaly here—invariably these apocalyptic images adorn buildings of the most noble solemnity and grandeur. The postmillennial world, as Glaber describes it, is not all guilt-ridden and downcast. It is also filled with optimism and hope. Maybe these graphic accounts of punishment and suffering found above countless medieval church doors and painted on walls should be seen not so much as moral judgments designed to terrify the illiterate sinner, but as a dire warning not to stray. More particularly, they appear to be a form of exorcism, of cleansing, akin to warding off the evil eye. They are the Devil's chorus deliberately placed there as a foil within a drama which is actually about celebration—celebrating the fact that humankind has proved itself able to withstand all such terrible temptations, and is permitted in the eyes of God to enter the New Jerusalem. And indeed, within two centuries this idea of an urban paradise, a city of God, was to find its ultimate expression in the soaring architecture of the Gothic cathedrals and the ecstatic sculpture that accompanied it.

The story of Cluny offers a solid corrective to the popular assumption that people always died young in the Middle Ages. Mayeul's successor as abbot, Odilo (St. Odilo), held office for nearly fifty-five years, while the man who followed him, Hugh of Semur (St. Hugh), was abbot for a full sixty years. It is a remarkable fact that the rule of the fifth and sixth abbots of Cluny spanned the entire eleventh century. And these were the years that saw Cluny at its greatest, although latterly at its most vulnerable.

Following the Cluniac tradition, Odilo was yet another aristocrat, though a lesser one compared to the grandeur which had surrounded Mayeul. Odilo's family came from the Auvergne, and the young man spent the first fifteen years of his monastic life at Baume-les-Messieurs, from where Cluny's first two abbots had emerged. Odilo took the abbot's throne in 994, not relinquishing it until his death on December 31, 1048. By that time he had been a monk for seventy years, which suggests that he must have been nearly ninety, perhaps even older, when he died.

The most remarkable quality about Odilo was his energy. He poured that energy into travel, into building projects on a huge scale, into the beautification of Cluny itself, into the campaign for the Christian reconquest of Spain from the Moors, and into the reform of yet more monasteries, which by now was taking place across the length and breadth of France. The laxity of religious houses at the time was widely felt—by both secular and church leaders—to be urgently in need of correction if Christendom was to possess the moral muscle required to confront the alien forces at its borders and within its midst; and there was no institution better equipped to perform such a service than Cluny. Monastic reform meant a strict imposition of Cluniac customs in all matters affecting a monk's daily life—from the nature and number of church services he was required to attend, to his food, clothing and personal morality—and all in strict accordance with the Rule set out by St. Benedict. And in order to ensure that such discipline was correctly observed the head of each reformed monastery or priory was made directly responsible to the abbot of Cluny himself who personally, though usually benevolently, held the reins of power in his hands.

Bishop Fulbert of Chartres once described Odilo as "the archangel of monks." Odilo's drive and achievements were awesome, and by his death there was no longer any doubt in the Christian world that Cluny was the most important monastery in Europe, and that its abbots were by now as powerful as the Holy Roman emperor and the pope—perhaps more influential in church matters than the Emperor, and certainly more politically powerful than the pope.

This extraordinary expansion, both in property and influence, was the direct result of the social and political condition of the times. While Cluny's very existence depended on the feudal structure of medieval society, with its rigidly defined class system reaching down from noblemen to serfs and slaves, it also lay above and apart from that feudal world, and therefore above and apart from its relentless quarrels and power struggles; and this was part of the abbey's huge strength. In addition to being able to offer moral security, Cluny could also act as a mediator in those quarrels.

These were generally over land ownership. At the very beginning of Odilo's abbacy two powerful French lords, Archambaud of Bourbon and Landry of Nevers, were in the throes of a bitter war over the possession of certain lands between the rivers Loire and Allier. The countryside was being devastated. Eventually, at a synod held at the Cluniac abbey of Sauxillanges in the Auvergne, a solemn agreement was sworn by a gathering of bishops and noblemen as well as representatives of people from the disputed lands, insisting that the conflict be brought to an end. A strongly worded deed was drawn up, later confirmed by two French archbishops, which began: "Since we know that without peace no man may see God, we adjure you, in the name of the Lord, to be men of peace...."

Hence there arose the institution that became known as the Pax Dei, the Peace of God. And Cluny's influence and authority lay at the heart of it. The abbots of Cluny became the brokers of peace, a kind of United Nations of its day, or, perhaps more accurately, the ombudsman. Not surprisingly, such a weight of moral authority invited rewards of a material kind, partly out of gratitude, partly self-interest. For the most part these rewards took the form of gifts from the aristocracy, the people who had most to give but also most to gain from the abbey's support. Donations, some of them lavish in the extreme, had begun to flow Cluny's way within a few decades of its foundation, slowly at first, but gradually increasing in number. In the year 921, while Cluny's first abbot, Berno, was still in office, a local count gave the abbey the church of Souvigny (near Moulins) along with its adjacent houses and fields, the water meadows in the valley, the vineyards on the nearby hillside, and the forests that rose above them. One reward the man received in return was the right for himself and his family to be buried within the walls of the abbey.

Gifts like these were fairly typical, and again it would be a gross oversimplification to pinpoint any single motive. Unquestionably the desire to be in the good books of those who had the ear of God would have played a large part; yet it would be unjust to overlook a more humble motive, particularly in such deeply religious times, namely the desire to give something for God in a true spirit of charity better expressed in the Latin *caritas*—"love," "esteem," "selfless giving." In 927 the nephew of Cluny's founder Duke William of Aquitaine gave the abbey a church his uncle had built at Sauxillanges along with the lands surrounding it. In 930 the Duke of Burgundy gave Cluny the important monastery of Romainmotier in the Jura. In all, by the end of the tenth century the abbey had received over 600 gifts of land, most of it agricultural and highly profitable.

And so it continued, the scale of gifts tending to become grander and grander. Abbot Mayeul became a close friend of the Holy Roman Emperor Otto I and his wife the Empress Adelaide. He stayed with them for lengthy periods at their court in northern Italy, and was rewarded for his attentions by being given one of the most ancient and celebrated monasteries in Italy, Sant'Apollinare in Classe in Ravenna, whose mosaic-covered church still stands as one of the nobler monuments in that city.

Exactly how Cluny managed to control and administer such a growing empire remains something of a mystery, though there can be no doubt that it did so. One answer has to lie in the bonds of loyalty that prevailed in feudal society. The monks of each house were bound to serve the abbot as they would a feudal lord, while the abbot, or prior, of each dependent house was directly answerable to the abbot of Cluny. In this way such a far-flung empire could be administered smoothly; the chain of authority had no weak links. But just in case there should be lapses in discipline, and a relapse into old slovenly ways, it was well known that the supreme authority, the abbot of Cluny himself, might at any time appear on one of his tireless journeys to check up on his domain.

Gifts and bequests redoubled in number under Abbot Odilo. The Empress Adelaide gave him the monastery of St. Victor in Geneva. The bishop of Autun donated the small monastery of Mesvres that lay close to his cathedral city. And in 1026 the great abbey of Vézelay, in northern Burgundy, came under Cluniac rule. A few years earlier, in 1014, the Holy Roman Emperor Henry II had visited Cluny at Odilo's invitation, and besides donating his personal estates in Alsace, as a measure of his respect for the place he decided to give the abbey his coronation orb, scepter and crown, as well as a cross of solid gold.

While donations of churches and monasteries added greatly to Cluny's prestige and power, financially the most lucrative gifts continued to be those of land. It is recorded that in the four-year period from 1027 to 1030 alone the abbey received no fewer than thirty-one such donations. One incident illustrates what was almost certainly not an unusual event. A local lord by the name of Guichard was brought to Cluny past speech and at the point of death. He was duly received by the monks and tended in the abbey's infirmary. His relatives, concerned for the salvation of the man's soul, promptly agreed to make the abbey a handsome donation of agricultural land in return for the monks' blessing and prayers.

Similar incidents, likewise recounted in the abbey's charters, indicate other frequent motives guiding the generosity of landowners. When a man chose to enter the abbey and take monastic vows he was expected to unburden himself of personal possessions; and while dukes and high-ranking lords could hardly be expected to shed their entire inheritance, a sizeable contribution of land and property would certainly ease his entry into the monastic community of his choice. Likewise, parents anxious to commit one of their children to the monastic life as an oblate, later to become a novice and ultimately a monk, would be required to make an appropriate gift to the abbey—and since most oblates came from the aristocracy rather than the peasantry, the most natural gift would be that of land.

Other motives were more raw, or more desperate. Men who had committed some grave crime, whether bigamy, theft, incest, or murder, might have managed to escape formal punishment, but not in the eyes of God; and as his own death loomed, only the prayers of the monks could save the wrongdoer from hellfire. And those prayers, and the absolution he longed for, came at a price—the donation of land. (In this context it is worth recalling that Cluny's own founder, Duke William of Aquitaine, had himself once committed a murder.)

Sometimes there might be a quid pro quo attached to such a donation. In 1013 a certain Atto offered Cluny possession of his serfs as well as woods and large areas of land in several villages, but only on the condition that the monks guarantee him all necessities of food and clothing for the remainder of his life. So, insurance of one kind or another, whether benevolent or selfish, seems to have been one key motive behind these multiple acts of generosity, another being genuine altruism and a desire to thank God for blessings received. And all of these motives, of course, made Cluny very rich.

Under Abbot Odilo in the first half of the eleventh century Cluny was at the very heart of things—in international diplomacy, in religious reform, in the conduct of the holy war in Spain, as well as in art, architecture, and music. Of his contribution to the abbey itself Odilo's boast was that he "had found it wood and left it marble." We get a glimpse of the new splendor of the place from a Roman cleric who was on a visit to Cluny in 1063 as part of the entourage of the papal legate Peter Damian. The Italian wrote with breathless amazement "how the great and vaulted church is furnished with numerous altars . . . and richly adorned with various precious things: how vast the cloister is and by its beauty seems to invite the monks to dwell there: how he [i.e., Odilo] has marvelously adorned the cloisters with columns and marble brought from the furthest part of the province." The astonished cleric was equally taken with the plumbing, remarking "how in all the offices, and wherever water is necessary, it marvelously flows at once and of its own accord from hidden channels"—a level of sanitation not found in Europe since Roman times.

But the richer and more prestigious the abbey became, and the greater its monastic empire, the more resentment was stirred up among diocesan authorities in Burgundy, who saw an ever-increasing number of church properties being removed from their jurisdiction, and fewer and fewer taxes coming their way as a result. In the early days, when the abbey had been no more than a small settlement in the woods, Cluny's exemption from all local interference, on which Duke William had insisted in his foundation charter, had been no more than a small dent in the pride of local bishops. But now, with its monastic family stretching far and wide across the land, and gifts and grants of property arriving in a torrent from feudal lords, the crisis was reaching the boiling point. The bishop of Laon was roused to describe the Cluniacs as "that warlike order of monks under their lord King Odilo." Even more hostile was the local bishop of Mâcon (as his successors were so often to be); in 1025 he even attempted to have Odilo excommunicated. Whatever his grounds were for claiming so drastic a penalty, they must have been serious enough for the abbot to hasten to Rome to state his case. Here he succeeded in obtaining from Pope John XIX a papal bull confirming all of Cluny's special rights—including the abbey's independence and freedom from all local interference, this privilege being further extended to embrace all Cluniac monks in all the connected monasteries and priories which were under the authority of the motherhouse.

The pope's verdict was seen as a stunning insult to church authorities in Burgundy, and not one they would easily forget. But Odilo was a natural diplomat, and played his cards skillfully. Ever since the Emperor Henry II had visited Cluny, the two had remained close, and Odilo maintained good relations with Henry's successors. As a result, he had powerful support on two sides—he had Europe's most important political patron, the emperor, as well as the most important spiritual patron, the pope. The local bishops had been outmaneuvered on both fronts. Moreover, Odilo's greatest strength lay in the knowledge that both the emperor and the pope needed the prestige and moral authority of Cluny. Before long the abbey was to play the honest broker to both sides.

It was about this time, early in the eleventh century, that all the monasteries which had been rigorously reformed by Cluny—right across France—came to be united within what was now identified as the Order of Cluny. Previously there had just been a loose arrangement of reformed monasteries that had become dependent on Cluny largely through donations. Now that dependency had been made official, and Cluny could operate as the acknowledged head of a separate church body under the broad embrace of the Benedictine Order. The Cluniac empire had become a highly-organized state within a state. The order, of Cluny was an administrative structure, with the motherhouse at its center. It was also a highly centralized and hierarchical system, in which all power and responsibility ultimately lay with the abbot. All monks in the outlying dependencies were expected to spend some time at Cluny. The superiors of dependent houses were subordinate to the head of Cluny itself, and this line of command—quite different from the other communities of the Benedictine order, which had a strong tradition of independence—gave enormous prestige to the motherhouse and its abbot, who was expected to enforce the centralized power structure and allegiance by regular visits to the daughter houses.

If the affairs of Cluny sometimes appear complacent and unduly materialistic, we get occasional glimpses of a harsher reality.

In 1033, the fortieth year of Odilo's rule, Raoul Glaber describes a disastrous famine in Burgundy in his *Historiae*. Three years of excessive rain had resulted in waterlogged fields. No plowing was possible. No crops could be sown. There was no grass for animals to graze on. There was no food to be had. People were dying like flies, and wolves were seen prowling in broad daylight about the towns and villages to prey on the unburied dead. Cannibalism had broken out. In the marketplace at Tournus, under the shadow of the abbey rebuilt by those Lombard craftsmen, a man had been caught offering human flesh for sale. The culprit had been hanged, and his body burned.

Glaber makes no comment on how Cluny, with its ever-increasing possessions of farmland and its healthy flow of rents, managed to survive, or at what sacrifice. One longs for more intimate diaries, or surviving letters of the kind that in the following century abound. But Cluny's role in the famine remains a tantalizing blank.

Nonetheless, even those sparse comments by Glaber serve to illuminate the raw nature of the times. The Rule of St. Benedict may have held sway within the abbey walls, but outside it was the rule of violence that tended to dominate people's lives. It is recorded that Odilo bravely attempted to impose what was called a "Truce of God" on Cluniac territory, forbidding all acts of violence between Wednesday evening and the following Monday morning. Again there is no evidence of how thoroughly the abbot's truce was respected, or whether aggressions were simply held in check for four and a half days until violence resumed between Monday afternoon and Wednesday morning.

Perhaps it is a mark of these violent times that the monks of Cluny should have begun to make a formal ceremony of offering prayers for the dead. About the year 1030 Odilo publicly proclaimed the second day of November each year to be designated All Souls' Day, a date in the church calendar which is still celebrated.

Odilo was a man with the restlessness of a zealot. For all the dangers of brigands, problems of communication, and roads that often had been scarcely attended to since the Roman legions departed, he made no fewer than nine journeys to Italy during his abbacy, spreading the gospel of reform among monasteries for whom the Rule of St. Benedict was often little more than a trace memory, if indeed they had ever heard of it. But the chief focus of his zeal was not Italy, but Spain. A century before the First Crusade and the goal of "liberating" the Holy Land, Christian eyes had become focused on the Iberian peninsula. It was here that Islam remained the most potent threat. Throughout the ninth and tenth centuries Moorish armies had repeatedly harried Christian lands, even driving north of the Pyrenees and deep into France. In 929 the caliphate of Córdoba had been established, politically independent of Baghdad and marking the fact that the epicenter of Islamic culture and military organization had now shifted west. Pamplona, capital of Navarre, had already fallen to the Moors. Finally, at more or less the moment when Odilo became abbot, Santiago de Compostela fell. It was only a brief period of conquest, scarcely more than a raid; but Santiago, so named after the apostle St. James the Greater who was supposedly buried there, was a shrine of special veneration, before long due to become the most esteemed place of pilgrimage in all of Europe.

This was Odilo's inheritance. And throughout the long years of his abbacy it was the Christian reconquest of Spain that was to remain his most burning ambition.

In the interests of this religious zeal it was, of course, extremely useful to be able to represent the Moors simply as barbarian invaders threatening the superior and God-fearing civilization of Christian Europe. And for the majority of those Burgundian knights who were to take up arms against Muslim Spain, it was precisely in such a light that they would have seen their enemy. On the other hand there would have been some—and Abbot Odilo would almost certainly have been one of them—who were capable of seeing the Moors in a different light: they might be presenting a grave challenge to Christendom militarily, but this was not the only challenge they offered. By the time Odilo became abbot of Cluny in 994 the Muslim civilization in southern Spain had already been

enjoying a golden age for more than a century. Culturally and intellectually—whether in the fields of music and literature, science and philosophy, architecture and craftsmanship, medicine or political thought—Muslim Spain, the kingdom of Al-Andalus, was infinitely more advanced than anything Christendom had to offer at this same period. The city of Córdoba, with a population of more than a million, was the sophisticated capital of a flourishing caliphate, a great center of trade and wealth as well as the seat of distinguished scholars, astronomers, poets, doctors, and historians, many of them Arabic-speaking yet Spanish in origin. Nothing in Christian Europe could compare artistically with Córdoba's Great Mosque, today known as the Mezquita, or with the caliphs' majestic royal city of Medina Azahara, still being developed and wonderfully embellished at the very moment that Odilo was dreaming of his holy war. The Great Mosque, built in the eight and ninth centuries, is one of the glories of the world, with its nineteen naves and row after row of delicate pillars and horseshoe-shaped arches.

But tragically it was not until much of Spain had been "liberated" by the Christian armies in the centuries to follow that Europe began to glean the benefit of that remarkable Moorish culture.

So it was under Odilo's abbacy that Cluny, with the support of the papacy, first used its prestige, its money, and its powerful feudal connections to come to the aid of the beleaguered Christian kingdoms in northern Spain. From the year 1017, and on into the next century, the abbots of Cluny are known to have promoted, or at the very least approved, no fewer than twenty military expeditions into the Iberian peninsula.

Not surprisingly, it was strongly in the interests of Spain's Christian rulers to become patrons of Cluny. The first to do so was King Sancho III of Navarre (called "the Great" for reasons that are not entirely clear). It was a well-timed alliance—the brilliant Moorish vizier and warlord Al-Mansur had died in the year 1002, after which the military incentive of Islam in the peninsula became noticeably weaker, so that King Sancho was soon able to extend his control over neighboring Aragon, Castile, and León—a sizeable part of northern Spain bordering on the Pyrenees and the Cantabrian mountains.

Sancho's relationship with Cluny maintained a fine balance between the military and the religious. Right up until his death in 1035 he kept in close touch with the abbot, both by exchange of letters and through visiting legates and ambassadors. He invited Cluniac monks to Spain, and in turn Cluny received and trained Spanish monks. One of these was a certain Paternus who arrived in Burgundy in 1025 and, having been duly instructed in the ways of Cluny, returned to Spain to become abbot of Cluny's first monastery south of the Pyrenees, San Juan de la Peña, near Jaca, in Navarre. Cluny's monastic empire was beginning to spread across country borders.

But it was as a reward for the abbey's support in the military field that Cluny benefited even more strongly from the Spanish connection. Exactly how active a role the abbey may have played in these military operations is uncertain, but we know for sure that King Sancho rewarded the abbey most handsomely for its efforts. In addition, the conquering knights also seem to have donated to the abbey quite generously. According to Raoul Glaber many of the spoils from defeated Moors in northern Spain were sent back by French knights to the abbey which had sponsored them, so supplementing the wealth of gifts already made by the grateful Sancho.

No wonder, then, that the Roman cleric who visited Cluny with the papal legate was astonished by the "great and vaulted church . . . richly adorned with various precious things," and by the many-columned cloisters. And no wonder, too, that towards the end of his life Abbot Odilo should have been able to boast of his Cluny that he "had found it wood and left it marble."

V.

Hugh the Great

The word "abbot" comes originally from the Aramaic *abba*, meaning "father." And in the long history of Cluny no title fitted a man more aptly than it did Abbot Hugh.

Hugh held the reins of power at Cluny for sixty years, from 1049 to 1109, and these were the years when the abbey and its empire were at their greatest. In the course of those six decades the number of religious houses dependent on Cluny throughout Europe rose from around sixty to between fifteen hundred and two thousand. And Hugh ruled them all—or at least he was the ultimate authority; no major decisions could be taken without his nod. His word was law. He was their feudal lord, their *abba*, and they were his vast family. It is tempting to see, in the concentration of so much power in the hands of a single man, the seeds of an inevitable decay, and events of the centuries to follow tend to justify this view—at least superficially. In reality, by the beginning of the twelfth century many other factors had come into play that had little or nothing to do with Abbot Hugh's personality or his absolute rule. All empires crumble in the end, victims of changing power structures or political climates, or simply internal fatigue and the relentless passage of time.

Cluny had its bright dawn, its long midday, and its even longer dusk. And with the accession of Hugh to the abbacy it was now approaching midday.

He is a man we know better by his deeds than by his personality, which we can do little more than deduce from the reactions of those around him. By the broadest of assessments Hugh was clearly quite extraordinary; no average human being could have built and controlled such an empire, retaining at the same time the respect, and often affection, of so many prominent men of the day whom he knew and worked with. The list is remarkable: it included nine successive popes, three Holy Roman emperors, and several kings of Spain and France, not to mention William the Conqueror in England with whom Hugh corresponded on church matters. In the course of that long life Hugh acted as counselor, mediator, guide, and trusted friend to the leaders of much of Europe.

Four biographies of Hugh survive, all of them written by fellow monks, one of them being a nephew who became an archbishop. The hagiographical embellishment of these biographies is reflective of the medieval mind.

At the same time we do actually know quite a lot about him. He was the eldest son of the local feudal lord, Count Dalmatius of Semur-en-Brionnais in southern Burgundy, and in Semur he was born in the year 1024, only a short distance from Cluny, which he would certainly have been aware of from a very early age. He was the oldest boy of at least ten children, including four brothers. The count had powerful connections; one of Hugh's sisters was to marry the Duke of Burgundy, brother of King Henry I of France (though the duke repudiated her four years later, so provoking a bitter quarrel in which Hugh's father was killed).

It was still a raw and crude world that Hugh of Semur was born into. Tales of feudal connections and feudal power can easily build up a picture of extravagant wealth and grandeur—a picture which would be entirely appropriate to Burgundy in the fifteenth and sixteenth centuries under the great dukes, but which bears no resemblance whatsoever to aristocratic life in the eleventh century as it would have been experienced by the young Hugh. The noble châteaux with their gilded state rooms, liveried servants by the legion, and acres of manicured parterres were things of a quite unimaginable future in those times, far beyond the dreams of even the most powerful local lord. In early medieval Burgundy there was little time for pomp and even less opportunity for displays of luxury. And Hugh's birthplace demonstrates this truth almost brutally.

In the center of the small country town of Semur stand the remains of his family's castle, or more accurately a keep, dating from the ninth century. A huddle of mean little rooms, courtyards, and narrow stairways leads eventually to an open space from which rises a freestanding circular tower, or what is left of it, a faceless hunk of stone some seventy-five feet in height with walls more than six feet thick at the base and an ugly gash down one side which has been left unrepaired for many centuries. The interior is bare and hollow, open to the sky and to a flock of raucous jackdaws.

Originally this tower consisted of five stories. A notice on the wall points out that there would have been a large open fireplace on the third floor, and this would have heated the floor above. All that remains today are deep niches round the wall, eight feet above your head and roughly a yard apart, which would once have carried the oak beams that supported the floor of the room above. This would have been just a single room—admittedly with underfloor heating and perhaps with partitions, but it was here that Count Dalmatius and his wife lived, and where Hugh was born and brought up, as presumably were the numerous younger siblings who followed him. Creature comforts can hardly have been among the benefits of being one of the most powerful figures in Burgundy.

Abbot Hugh was to become one of the great builders of all time. It is tempting to imagine that his childhood experience of so

grim an environment may have fired his determination to build for glory and for God regardless of cost.

As son and heir, Hugh was of course expected to take his due place in the family hierarchy, beginning in the approved way by being trained as a knight. But even as a boy he had quite other ideas, insisting that he was rather unsuited to a martial role and that he intended instead to enter the church and eventually to become a monk at Cluny. For a while Count Dalmatius fiercely opposed his son's decision. In the end he gave his reluctant consent, and Hugh at the age of fourteen entered the monastery of St. Marcel at Chalon-sur-Saône, which had been given to Cluny as a dependency by Hugh's great-uncle together with his grandfather. And from St. Marcel three years later he entered the abbey of Cluny, becoming first a deacon and then a priest, probably by the age of twenty.

Hugh was described at that time as being tall, well built, physically striking, and deeply pious. He was also regarded as austere, but at the same time warmly human. People liked him, and were perhaps rather in awe of this young nobleman who had apparently given up so much to serve the church. Before long he evidently showed outstanding qualities as an administrator, because the aged Abbot Odilo appointed Hugh grand prior of the abbey when he was still only twenty-two years of age. Two years later he was entrusted to conduct church business in Germany, and it was while he was away that Odilo died—after having ruled Cluny for over half a century.

On February 20, 1049, on his return from Germany, Hugh was enthroned as abbot. He was twenty-four. And no one was more proud than his father, Count Dalmatius. He could now bask in the glory of having a child who had suddenly been elevated to one of the most prestigious seats of office the feudal world could offer. The count's family had overnight climbed several rungs on the social ladder.

From now onwards Hugh would be a power in the land, or rather, a power in several lands, for his was an authority that transcended national boundaries just as it transcended national interests. Perhaps, not unlike the secretary-general of the United Nations today, the abbot of Cluny saw his role as a universal and benevolent one which carried the huge moral authority of being impartial. Hugh could be everyone's referee.

Ironically, this man who was to attract such a phenomenal quantity of property and goods to the cause of Cluny managed to do so from the platform of being spiritually above all such material things. All the same it was inevitable that possessing this kind of authority would very soon draw Hugh into international politics, and in particular into the most vicious political battle of the day. This was the unyielding tug-of-war between the Holy Roman emperors in Germany and the popes in Rome for the leadership of the Christian world. Both sides claimed it, the emperor by right of possession and right of history (as the natural heir of Charlemagne), the pope by divine right as bishop of Rome and the rightful heir of St. Peter and St. Paul. For the abbot of Cluny, his role was a balancing act—it was as though the fates had handed Hugh the task of reconciling the impossible.

The first warning came right at the beginning, in the very month of Hugh's election as abbot. A German bishop by the name of Bruno of Egisheim (sometimes called Bruno of Toul) was enthroned in Rome as Pope Leo IX. He was a man of nearly fifty, with an impressive and honorable record as a reformer in the service of the church, and he had been appointed to the papacy by the emperor Henry III. The German emperors, precisely because they regarded themselves as the heirs of Charlemagne, considered the papacy to be an appointment within their gift. Popes were simply "bishops of Rome," useful, but at all times subservient. In fact Henry III, during a colorful reign, managed to appoint no fewer than three popes, as well as depose three more. Doubtless he saw Leo, a relative of his, as an authoritative but essentially pliant man in the Vatican, an easy tool who would certainly give him no trouble. This was the beginning of what turned out to be a massive error of judgment on the part of the emperor.

Pope Leo IX has become known as the first of the great reforming popes of the Middle Ages. He was a man who not only strengthened the office of pope itself, hitherto morally lax and frequently corrupt, but who also began the process of establishing the papacy as the principal authority within the Roman Catholic Church. Inevitably this brought him into direct conflict with the emperor who had appointed him, and the conflict broke out immediately. Leo insisted on seeking the approval of the clergy of Rome before being enthroned, a gesture clearly intended to demonstrate his opposition to lay authority, and in particular his opposition to the authority of the emperor. In fact it amounted to a serious snub. Relations between the two men deteriorated thereafter. The issue that soon came to divide them most hotly was the sensitive one of lay investitures—church appointments made by secular rather than ecclesiastical authorities. Henry maintained that it was his right, as Holy Roman emperor, to appoint bishops and other senior clergy as he wished. This, he argued, was what emperors were there for, and what they had always done. Pope Leo, on the other hand, insisted that no lay authority had any such right: these were spiritual appointments and could only be made by someone with spiritual authority. A storm was brewing—the pope was inviting the wrath of the most powerful political figure of the day.

Abbot Hugh's involvement in this issue was almost accidental to begin with. He was one of a number of bright young churchmen with whom Pope Leo chose to keep regular contact. The link between the two men was also a historical one, because of Cluny's direct obedience to Rome. Cluny needed the protection of the papacy, and the pope needed the support of Cluny.

But there were other allegiances as well. Since its foundation Cluny had developed strong ties with the German emperors; in 1051 Hugh received a letter from Henry III inviting him to be godfather to his infant son and heir, the future Henry IV. This was not an invitation to refuse, and so later that year Hugh rode to the imperial residence in Cologne with a small entourage to become the personal guest of the emperor and to help officiate in the baptism of Henry's son. As a result Hugh now had binding loyalties to both pope and emperor. Eventually the competing pressures would prove to be unbearable.

International affairs occupied a large slice of Hugh's life. He traveled tirelessly, even crossing the Alps several times in midwinter. His retinue was always modest, consisting of two or three officials from the abbey, a personal groom, and a few servants. On the other hand, on his return to Cluny he would be received by a formal procession of all the monks, singing, and no doubt bowing to him as he passed. Hugh had a taste for ceremony, and he was especially fond of ritual.

Order, and orderly routine, was the essential key to the monastic life at Cluny, as Hugh perceived it to be. In a generally disorderly world this precise compartmentalizing of the daily routine helped make the cloistered life one of enviable stability. Much of that stability was generated by the communal nature of life at Cluny. For all the growing power and wealth of the place, there were few individual privileges to be enjoyed. Hugh, this man of such great authority and prestige, slept in a common dormitory like any other monk; there was no abbot's house at Cluny until the twelfth century. He also took his meals in the company of the other monks in the refectory, though latterly he did have his own separate table. Traditionally the abbots of Cluny took their turn in the kitchen along with a rota of monks, usually four of them at a time for a period of a week, though it does seem unlikely that Hugh would have found the time in his busy schedule to perform these daily chores.

But there was always time in Cluny for ritual—daily life in the abbey was controled by it. Whether it was the total silence observed throughout the period of Christmas, or the daily reading of a chapter of the Rule of St. Benedict in the chapter house (hence its name), every hour, every day, every season at Cluny had its all-controling ritual and ceremony. There were already forty-eight feast days observed each year by the time Hugh became abbot, and to this number he proceeded to add six more. Some of these demanded considerable stamina: at the festival of St. Peter and St. Paul, the abbey's patron saints, the night office began at dusk on June 28 and continued unbroken until daybreak on June 29. Altogether there was a steady increase in ceremonies surrounding the abbot's person throughout his years in office, a reflection of his own prestige as well as that of the abbey.

There was a magnificence about this ceremonial life, with its resplendent church services, the increasing wealth of ornament and decoration throughout the abbey, and the ever-more-elaborate chanting of psalms that continued day and night, which left all who attended it with a feeling of awe, as if they had been awarded a glimpse of another world, perhaps a glimpse of heaven on earth.

Yet this dominance of ritual had its critics, and before long—not surprisingly—there would be voices raised outside the abbey that Cluny was losing its way, that it had already lost sight of those humble ideals which St. Benedict had endeavored to pursue when he founded Monte Cassino and wrote the Rule. In other words, in becoming devoted exclusively to the love of ceremony, was Cluny falling in love with itself?

And where, its critics wondered, was God in all this?

VI.

Spanish Excursions

A key factor in Cluny's expansion under Abbot Hugh was that many of its new dependencies rapidly acquired dependencies of their own, so vastly multiplying the possessions of the motherhouse. The priory of Notre Dame at La Charité, for example, on the western borders of Burgundy, was founded in the early years of Hugh's abbacy and very soon acquired no fewer than seventy dependencies in dioceses as far away as Chartres, Sens, Rouen, and ultimately in England. La Charité became known as "the eldest daughter of Cluny." Then there was St. Martin-des-Champs in Paris, placed under Cluniac rule somewhat later, in 1079. It likewise expanded considerably until the priory came to embrace more than thirty other houses, becoming effectively the Cluny of the north.

And at Marcigny, only a few miles from his home town of Semur, Hugh founded the first Cluniac nunnery. It is easy to assume in this male-oriented world that the spiritual welfare of women was of little concern. But for the Cluniacs this was not so. Marcigny became the first of many such institutions for women. It was entirely a family venture, established on family lands with the collaboration of Hugh's brother Geoffrey, and its first prioress was their own sister, by the name of Ermengarde. As was usually the case with Hugh's enterprises, multiple endowments soon came its way, and before long there was provision at Marcigny for a maximum of ninety-nine nuns—the one hundredth being the invisible presence of the Virgin Mary, for whom a special pew was always reserved in church as well as a place laid at every meal.

But a large number of Cluny's new dependencies, either founded or else acquired by Hugh, were designed to fulfill a very special function, one that was particularly close to Hugh's heart. Leyrac, Moissac, Auch, Figeac, Eauze, Toulouse, Saintes, Limoges, St. Jean d'Angély, St. Gilles—these were abbeys or priories situated along some of the principal roads leading to the Pyrenees, and therefore toward Spain. In origin they were Roman roads, built for military and trading purposes, but more recently they had come to perform a quite different role. Now they were pilgrim roads, threading their way across the French countryside like a giant spider web, only to merge into a single principal road south of the Pyrenees in Navarre, which then struck westwards across northern Spain through Castile, León, and Galicia until reaching its final destination towards the end of the then known world, close to the Atlantic Ocean. Here was the shrine, and supposedly the grave, of the martyred apostle St. James in the city that became named after him, Santiago de Compostela. This was the pilgrims' ultimate goal, their supreme object of veneration.

The popularity of Santiago as a sacred site was second to no other in much of the Middle Ages. Now that the Christian reconquest of Spain had begun, and the journey no longer led through Muslim lands, more than half a million people are reckoned to have taken that road to St. James's city each year by the eleventh century. It was the long road to heaven, a means of obtaining absolution, *remissio peccatorum*, the remission of a person's sins. People went as a form of penance, or as punishment for a crime, as well as for a variety of more adventurous reasons, some more honorable than others. They would certainly have been a mixed bunch, and undoubtedly a colorful one. The journey might take six months in all or even longer. Pilgrims would leave their homes all over Europe in early spring, hope to arrive in Santiago in high summer, stay awhile to rest, pray, and drink thin Galician wine, then return home in the late autumn (assuming they had managed to survive the bandits and the cutthroats, the wolves and the bears) proudly clutching their *compostelle*, their certificate proving that they really had been there.

The story of the great pilgrimage of the Middle Ages is a heroic and moving one. The legend of St. James has been the stuff of dreams, wonderful, fanciful, implausible, at times downright deceitful; yet somehow the enormous appeal of that legend lit a path across medieval Europe which is still flagged by some of the brightest achievements of Europe's civilization—cathedrals, abbeys, carvings, paintings, civic architecture, as well as songs, poetry, and narratives of every kind. And in each chapter of the Santiago story is the hand of Cluny, and in particular that of Abbot Hugh. Without Cluny there might well have been no pilgrimage at all.

According to the legend of Santiago, the Apostle James (the Greater, cousin of Jesus, not to be confused with James the Lesser) responded to Christ's last command that his disciples fan out across the earth and evangelize far and wide. He spent several years attempting (without much success) to spread the gospel in Spain, before returning to Jerusalem and becoming the second Christian martyr, after St. Stephen, beheaded by a Roman sword around A.D. 44. His body, so the story goes, was then transported by two loyal disciples on a ship down the length of the Mediterranean and up the Atlantic coast as far as the Bay of Padrón in northwest Spain, where it was buried in a stone coffin on a remote hillside. Nothing further was heard of the matter for nearly eight centuries, by which time this lost corner of Europe had become a remote outpost of Christianity besieged by the armies of Islam.

At this critical moment the location of the apostle's tomb was miraculously revealed to a local hermit through the agency of a star accompanied by celestial music. Hearing of this discovery, the local king hastened to the tomb and pronounced that St. James was henceforth to be worshiped as the protector of Spain. He ordered a church and a small monastery to be built nearby, and before long these expanded into the settlement known as Campus Stellae (the Field of the Star), later shortened to Compostela. (Considerable doubt hangs over this interpretation of the name; it has also been interpreted as a diminutive of the Latin *componere*, to bury—in other words it could have meant a burial ground.)

This was only the beginning. Legend has it that from the ninth century onwards St. James began to appear on battlefield after battlefield as a mounted knight in shining armor, personally fighting the forces of the Islamic foe. He was Santiago Matamoros, "St. James the Moor-slayer." Allegedly he even appeared at the side of Spain's great military hero, El Cid, at Coimbra in the eleventh century—at the very time when Abbot Hugh was becoming deeply involved in the affairs of Spain and the cause of the reconquest.

Cluny and the great pilgrimage are inextricably linked. The driving force behind Hugh's ambitions in Spain, like that of Abbot Odilo before him, was the determination to push back Islam and so try to reclaim the Iberian peninsula for Christianity, and the huge popularity of the Santiago pilgrimage made it a perfect vehicle for these ambitions. The Cluniac abbeys and priories established by Hugh along the tributary roads in France acted as way stations for pilgrims heading for the Pyrenees. In a generally bleak and unsafe world monasteries were crucial for travelers both rich and poor, offering a safe house, a bed for the night, a meal, a prayer, a psalm.

They also provided the comfort of company, encouragement to press on, information about where to make for next, even medical help if need be.

Hugh now set about establishing a similar chain of priories right across northern Spain. Politics and pilgrimage came together. This was still a largely untamed land, dangerous and sparsely inhabited, and nothing less than a powerful network of religious houses, well equipped and well endowed, could offer pilgrims the kind of security and support they needed. As a result the Christian hold on northern Spain, and in particular the influence of Cluny and its reforms, became enormously increased. And the financial rewards were proportionately great. The noble and the wealthy joined the pilgrimage, and donations, gifts, bequests duly poured in. For Cluny, as well as for all others involved in servicing the great journey, the pilgrim roads to Santiago became a lucrative investment.

That Hugh succeeded in achieving all this was to a large extent due to a remarkable relationship he managed to cultivate between Cluny and a dynasty of Spanish rulers. These were men who were shockingly unscrupulous in their political dealings; nonetheless, they saw in the activities of the great French abbey a shared ambition, the reestablishment of Christianity south of the Pyrenees. Religion and political self-interest marched conveniently hand in hand.

The bond between Cluny and these Spanish rulers had been forged originally under Abbot Odilo. But now it began to gather strength year by year; to those ambitious Spanish monarchs Cluny's involvement came as a salvation of their own political lives. And in an abundance of gratitude they proceeded to reward the abbey with gold and properties—in huge quantities.

Cluny's first Spanish benefactor had been King Sancho III of Navarre. Then, after Sancho's death in 1035, his son Ferdinand I made the first of what was to become an annual grant of gold to Cluny in return for the abbey's continuing services to the *Reconquista*. This was in 1038, eleven years before Hugh became abbot. Not surprisingly, King Ferdinand was among the very first patrons to whom the young Hugh made diplomatic contact on taking office.

Yet this was only the start, and gifts to Cluny from Spain were soon to take on the proportions of a gold rush. Meanwhile, in the ruling house of northern Spain the family tradition of treachery and murder was being robustly maintained. When Ferdinand himself died in 1065 his three sons each inherited a slice of their father's kingdom. Sancho, *El Fuerte*, obtained Castile. The second brother, Alfonso VI, received León. And the youngest, García, was left with far-distant Galicia, which nevertheless included Santiago de Compostela.

Even as the gifts to Cluny continued to flow, what followed may well have caused Abbot Hugh some moments of uneasy conscience. Sancho and Alfonso were soon at one another's throats, each striving to grab the other's territory. In the ensuing battles Sancho gained the upper hand largely because his campaign was conducted by a brilliant mercenary general by the name of Rodrigo Díaz—the legendary El Cid. Alfonso was captured and thrown into prison. Sancho, however, had the misfortune to have a dream in which St. Peter appeared to him and urged him to release his royal captive, which he proceeded to do, whereupon Alfonso, in a display of brotherly sentiment, murdered him.

As a result, by the year 1072 Alfonso VI now ruled both León and Castile, just as his father had done, attributing this happy turn of events to the prayers of the monks of Cluny, one of whose patron saints after all was St. Peter. And in 1073 he took Galicia from his brother García, thus becoming the most powerful Christian ruler in Spain.

Four years later, in 1077, Hugh made his first visit to Spain to meet his royal benefactor. We have no record of precisely what occurred between them; nonetheless subsequent events leave little doubt that the substance of their meeting was a vigorous reaffirmation of Cluny's support for the church in Spain. At the same time it must also have been a council of war. Both strategies rode happily in harness. Alfonso's enthusiasm for Cluny found expression not only in lavish gifts of gold but in equally lavish gifts of priories and monasteries, especially those that lined the pilgrim road to Santiago de Compostela. Many of these became subsequently rebuilt or greatly expanded, their churches being modeled on the mother church (Cluny II).

At the same time, the pilgrim road itself, the *Camino de Santiago*, continued to be improved and made safer for travelers. Villages grew into towns, hostels and hospices sprung up, and an infrastructure developed to support the ever-increasing number of pilgrims using the road. Bridges started to replace fords, quite a few of which are still in use today. One of the finest of these, designed specially for pilgrims, was built at the command of King Alfonso's daughter Urraca, and it strides—almost swaggers—across the River Arga on the edge of the town in Navarre which is named after the bridge and the royal lady who built it: Puente la Reina, the Bridge of the Queen.

The most valuable of Cluny's new possessions came as a gift from Alfonso VI shortly after Hugh's first visit to Spain. This was the ancient abbey of Sahagún, situated on the dusty plain between Burgos and León, and already one of the key links in the chain of monasteries that serviced the pilgrim road. Today little about Sahagún hints at its former glory. All that remains, within stumps of ancient walls like broken teeth, is the gaunt, semiruined brick chapel of San Marco that was once attached to the great abbey. But in its heyday Sahagún became effectively the Cluny of Spain, with a Cluniac monk as its abbot and at least fifty other monasteries and priories dependent upon it. All in all, the addition of Sahagún represented a massive expansion of the Cluniac empire. It also stands as one of Hugh's major diplomatic triumphs, one that was promptly sealed by the award—personally given in Rome to Abbot Bernard of Sahagún from Pope Gregory VII—of many of the same lucrative privileges that Cluny itself already enjoyed. In this way the papacy and Cluny hugely increased their power and influence in Spain, while King Alfonso was happy to bask in the support of both.

In 1085 Alfonso conquered one of the key cities of Moorish Spain, Toledo, and in gratitude for Cluny's support Alfonso proceeded to express his gratitude to Hugh by doubling his father's annual tribute from one thousand pieces of gold to two thousand. This was a truly colossal sum, and what is more, this was not even a ceiling figure with a fixed end date.

No wonder Hugh now began to fulfill his greatest dream— his new abbey church (Cluny III), planned to be the largest church in Christendom. And within two years work had begun to bring this dream to life.

But in 1086 Alfonso's army was defeated at Sagrajas by an invading force of Almoravids from North Africa, and soon the king found himself short of funds. Hitherto much of Alfonso's generosity towards Cluny had been funded by loot seized from reconquered territories. Suddenly there was no such loot. As a result the annual tribute to Cluny began to fall seriously into arrears, so threatening the suspension of building work on the magnificent new abbey church that had begun to rise. Hugh's second visit to Spain, in 1090, was therefore more supplicatory than the first. He desperately needed a return to the status quo. Again we have no record of what passed between the two men, but we know that work did continue on the abbey church. Once again, it seems, Hugh's powers of persuasion must have prevailed.

More than forty years were to pass before Hugh's dream came to be realized and his "New Jerusalem" stood completed. By that time Hugh himself was long dead, as were his two immediate successors. It would fall to the last great abbot of Cluny to witness that moment of triumph when the abbey church was finally dedicated by Pope Innocent II in 1130. But in the years between the abbey continued to find itself, as always, center stage in the turbulent theater that was Europe.

VII.

Power and Politics

 Under Abbot Hugh the monastery of Cluny became the hub of a wheel whose spokes extended to every country in Europe, and before long as far as the Holy Land. His personal influence was of a kind hard to measure in modern terms. Hugh's feudal and family connections may find their equivalent in the workings of diplomatic and commercial coteries of our own day, where *whom* one knows may be more important than *what* one knows; but there can be no equivalent of the kind of moral weight that the abbot of Cluny could bring to bear upon international disputes and the squabbles of kings and princes in medieval Europe. Popes and Holy Roman emperors regularly claimed such authority; unfortunately the German emperors were too often at loggerheads with their own princelings to have much spare time for spiritual matters, while the papacy at this period in history was still too politically weak to have the clout to enforce that authority.

Only the monasteries, and above all Cluny (at least until the rise of the Cistercians), were sufficiently removed from the crude realities of worldly events, and sufficiently unblemished in their dedicated way of life, to be able to command that moral high ground.

Hugh's list of autocrats to whom he found himself acting as advisor is an impressive one. All of them were power-crazed bullies in different ways, and the role Hugh was repeatedly required to play on their behalf demanded an exceptional degree of tact along with a great deal of political acumen. Chief among them was Cluny's principal protector, Pope Gregory VII, himself a former Benedictine monk, though probably not at Cluny. Elected pope in 1073, Gregory was a man of single-minded nature given to frenetic outbursts. These tirades Hugh somehow managed to duck, while still apparently remaining on affectionate terms with the pontiff. Then there was the Spanish king Alfonso VI who in addition to being Cluny's principal benefactor had now also become Hugh's cousin by marriage. There was also the Holy Roman emperor, Henry IV, Hugh's godson, a handsome and charismatic man by all accounts, of whom Hugh was apparently deeply fond, but who was forever embarrassing his godfather not so much by his famous promiscuity (which in any case was little different from the behavior of most rulers of the day) as by repeatedly being excommunicated by the pope for insisting on exercising church privileges which Gregory had firmly denied him.

Closer to home was the French king, Philip I, another turbulent figure who managed to be excommunicated even more often than the Holy Roman emperor. Philip was a man thoroughly loathed by just about everyone in his own lands; his behavior to his people was more that of a robber baron than a monarch. Among his more spectacular misdemeanors was to have dismissed his legitimate wife only to kidnap the wife of the count of Anjou. It was towards the end of Hugh's life, when Philip had been king of France for forty-five years, that he wrote to the abbot inquiring whether ruling monarchs could become monks. Hugh in reply suggested that Philip resign his earthly kingdom, change his life, repent his sins, and become a monk at Cluny—an invitation which the French king declined to take up.

Maybe the most intriguing figure among the various rulers who touched on Hugh's life was William, duke of Normandy. This was the title by which Hugh first knew of him. Then, seventeen years after becoming abbot, he found himself required to address William as king of England. Whether Hugh actually met William the Conqueror is debatable, though it was claimed by an early biographer of Hugh that a meeting did take place during one of the abbot's visits to Normandy. Certainly the two men communicated over a number of years, both by letter and through legates and ambassadors. William was always the supplicant in this relationship, seeking Hugh's advice on church matters and begging him to send Cluniac monks to England. Hugh for his part kept the Conqueror at a cautious distance, treating him somewhat loftily as an upstart who was also, after all, illegitimate.

Hugh's way of maintaining good relations with such a disparate and willful bunch of men seems to have been to handle them with the most gentle of gloved hands, accompanied at the same time by a steely confidence in his own moral authority, a confidence no doubt born of an awareness that the voice of an abbot of Cluny carried a weight equal to that of any other figure in Christendom, if not indeed greater.

Of all the high-ranking figures of the day who featured prominently in Hugh's life none was more crucial to the well-being of Cluny than Pope Gregory VII. The abbey's special relationship with the papacy stemmed from its original foundation charter, but that relationship had grown warmer and more vibrant once the papal throne became occupied by a series of men who had themselves been Benedictine monks and who therefore shared many of Cluny's ideals of a reformed religious life. Gregory was perhaps the most worldly and ambitious of all the medieval popes; of the nine occupants of the papacy with whom Hugh had to deal in the course of his abbacy none was more intransigent. Gregory was a volatile man, a German from a relatively humble background who went to Rome at an early age, where he became a monk before returning to Germany. There he rose to power largely through his own labors, never managing to come to terms with the privileged and aristocratic world in which most of his contemporary church leaders lived. This made him an isolated figure in the echelons of power, and as a politician frequently a disaster: his career led him in and out of exile and from one dramatic confrontation to another—with the Holy Roman emperor, with various Italian warlords, as well as with the kings of France and Spain. Nonetheless, his admiration and affection for Abbot Hugh was genuine and deeply felt. Gregory saw himself as a spiritual leader above all, not as a statesman; and he saw in Cluny, which as a papal legate he had visited several times as a younger man, a model of the ideal spiritual life, and its abbot as the perfect guide and mentor for those leading that life.

The two men were old friends; as young church delegates they had a number of times been traveling companions to various reform councils. Long journeys on horseback would have given them plenty of opportunity to get to know each other well. Theirs seems to have been a friendship of opposites. They could hardly have been more different in character and temperament—the aristocratic Hugh was the quintessential statesman, while the self-made Gregory was the belligerent activist whose favorite quotation was from Jeremiah, "Cursed is he who keeps back his sword from blood."

A testimony to their friendship is the number of affectionate anecdotes relating to the two of them that must have originated from Gregory's early visits to Cluny, and which continued to circulate in the abbey long after the death of both men. Gregory enjoyed describing Hugh as *blandum tyrannum*—the urbane tyrant, "urbane" referring to his skill at handling people, and "tyrant" to his insistence on his own unchallengeable authority within the bounds of his abbey.

The two men met less frequently later in life, and Hugh visited Gregory in Rome only twice. Yet they communicated by letter regularly, and amid the political turbulence that swept through Gregory's years in office the pope seems to have found comfort and security in his relationship with Hugh. The image of monastic peace and tranquility must have seemed like heaven on earth to the beleaguered pontiff. There is an endearing warmth in his letters, as well as a note of despairing loneliness as he struggled to maintained his authority in Rome while it was becoming assailed on all sides. A letter of May 7, 1078 begins so touchingly: "Wearied by the pressure of all manner of people and by dealing with so many matters of business, I am writing a little to one I love much."

But then the mood could change and the bullish autocrat would come to the fore. Within a year he was writing to Hugh in a mood of severe rebuke. The issue was a political one: Hugh had welcomed the duke of Burgundy to Cluny as a monk. This was in itself nothing unusual—in the aristocratic world of medieval monasticism noblemen, even royalty, frequently chose to end their days in the quiet of a monastery where they would be in the company of friends and family, and where no one would expect them to obey the Rule of St. Benedict to the letter. But on this occasion Gregory saw red, and his reaction was a demonstration of his essentially feudal and embattled view of the Christian world. "You have taken or received the duke into the peace of Cluny," he wrote, "so that a hundred thousand Christians will be without a protector." It was not clear from Gregory's accusation what he imagined such a vast number of Burgundian Christians needed protection from—whether it was the Devil or invading armies.

In most of Gregory's battles the abbot of Cluny could do little more than be a witness, offering advice from time to time, pouring oil on troubled waters, striving as best he could to prevent the fiery pontiff from committing political suicide, which he appeared bent on doing. But then Gregory was not a man who understood the meaning of compromise. The crucial tenet of his interpretation of the papacy was his insistence that the spiritual leadership of Christendom rested with the pope rather than with the Holy Roman emperor. He maintained that the church was a kind of monarchy—an elective monarchy—and that the pope was therefore the monarch of that church, and accordingly superior to all other Christian leaders, however politically powerful they might be. The emperor's role was to be the guardian of the church, but not its ruler.

The significance of such a claim is huge; and it grows and multiplies as we place it in the context of the centuries to come, because in effect it began the process of separating church from state. However, the grounds upon which Gregory rested his claim were very far from solid. The authority he quoted was a document entitled the Donation of Constantine, in which the emperor Constantine, on establishing the city of Constantinople as the capital of the Eastern empire, voluntarily relinquished his temporal power over the Western empire in favor of the bishops of Rome. However, unknown to Gregory—at least we may charitably assume it was unknown to him—this Donation of Constantine was actually a forged document. In reality Gregory had no historical authority whatever to support his claim to be superior to the emperor. He was, strictly speaking, merely the bishop of Rome.

The emperor, on the other hand, claimed to be the leader of the Christian world as the heir of the former Roman emperors, with all their rights, both political and spiritual. This role had been repeatedly confirmed; in the mid-tenth century Otto the Great had been crowned in Rome as the rightful successor of Augustus, Constantine, and Charlemagne. And in the early eleventh century Conrad II had crossed the Alps to be crowned king of the Italians in Milan, followed by his coronation as emperor by the pope himself in Rome.

At the heart of the battle was the question of lay investiture; Gregory insisted that no lay authority had the right to appoint bishops and other high officers of the church. The issue had been fought about over twenty years before between Pope Leo IX and Emperor Henry III, and it had rumbled on unresolved ever since. But the present protagonists were men of much more fiery temperament; a head-to-head clash was inevitable. And it duly took place in the year 1077, in northern Italy, at a place whose name carries an epic ring: Canossa.

And in that famous encounter Abbot Hugh was to find himself positioned uneasily between both men. The pope was his friend and spiritual mentor, as well as being the sole guarantor of Cluny's privileges. But the emperor was also a friend and, in addition, was Hugh's godson.

The first sparks flew in 1075. The pope's Roman synod of that year came out damningly against the practice of lay investiture by the emperor, on the strength of which Gregory promptly excommunicated five of Henry's chief advisers. The emperor's response was contemptuous and bristling with aggression. He offered active support to the antireform faction in Milan and proceeded to replace the legitimate bishop of that city with his own appointee, adding further insult by appointing two more bishops at Spoleto and Fermo. The following year he rejected Gregory's offer to meet and sort out their differences, declaring instead—true to his family tradition—that the pope should now consider himself deposed. Gregory's response was a powerful one: he excommunicated the emperor.

As he heard of these developments Abbot Hugh set out to intervene. He traveled to Germany, possibly at the request of Gregory, in an attempt to mediate between the protagonists. But, excommunicated though he might be, Henry was in no mood for peace. Whatever Hugh's advice was, it fell on deaf ears. The emperor and the pope remained at daggers drawn.

Yet, for all Henry's belligerence the excommunication did begin to have an effect. An increasing number of German nobles and bishops withdrew their loyalty to him until the defection finally reached the point where it was decided that Henry would be deposed as emperor if he failed to receive absolution from the pope before February 22, 1077, the first anniversary of the papal sentence against him. Henry's German foes invited Gregory to meet them in Augsburg a few weeks before that final date in order to decide the emperor's fate.

Characteristically Henry realized that now was the time for desperate action: it was vital that he reach the pope before his hostile bishops and nobles could do so. This meant traveling to Italy without delay, by crossing the Alps in what was now midwinter. To make matters worse for Henry all Alpine passes leading southwards from Germany had been deliberately blocked by order of his enemies. Only one route remained open to him, by way of what is now French Savoie, to the northeast of Grenoble, and this meant tough negotiations (sweetened by a huge payment) before he obtained permission to take the route. Accordingly, shortly after Christmas 1076 the emperor, accompanied by his wife and family, as well as a large retinue, made for the Mont Cenis Pass, a hazardous journey over the Alps that few imagined they would ever manage.

For once we know what actually happened, because a lengthy account of that journey survives, written by a German monk named Lampert of Hersfeld in his *Annales*. "It was a very bitter winter," he wrote,

> and the lofty mountains which he had to cross were so covered with snow and ice that neither horse not human foot could take a step on the steep and slippery slopes without danger. But the anniversary of the king's excommunication drew near and would suffer no delay, since unless he could be absolved from anathema before that day he knew that his cause would be lost forever, and his kingdom forfeit. . . . So he hired local experts in Alpine passes to guide him up the steep mountain and over the drifts of snow. . . . With great difficulty they reached the summit, but they could get no further because the slippery ice seemed to deny any possibility of descent. But straining every nerve, now scrambling on hands and feet, now leaning on the shoulders of their guides, now staggering and slipping and falling, sometimes in grave danger, they just managed to reach the plains below. The queen and other ladies in their company were sat on ox-hides and dragged down by the leaders of the company.

Meanwhile Gregory was already making his way northwards to keep his appointment with the German princes. As soon as he heard of the emperor's movements he accepted the suggestion of one of his most powerful supporters, the countess Matilda of Tuscany, that he stay at her stronghold at Canossa, in Lombardy, and there await the arrival of Henry.

The stage was now set for the great confrontation.

Lampert is fairly verbose on the subject of the early negotiations and horse-trading which took place through the exchange of messengers and ambassadors. But one thing he fails to explain is why the third key occupant of the castle of Canossa at that moment, in addition to Pope Gregory and the Countess Matilda, should be the abbot of Cluny. We do not even know for certain who invited him to be present at such a crucial event in church history. Most likely the invitation came from the emperor, Henry's most urgent hope being that his prestigious godfather would prove to be the one man capable of having some influence on an intransigent pope.

Lampert described Henry's next move: "He came as was commanded; and since the castle was protected by a triple wall, he was received within the second circuit; stripped of his royal robes, with nothing kingly about him, entirely without display, barefoot, fasting from morning until evening he awaited the judgment of the pope. A second day he did it, then a third; eventually on the fourth he was admitted to the presence, and after much discussion, finally absolved."

No correspondence between Hugh and Pope Gregory survives relating to events at Canossa. There is just one account which claims that it was Hugh who intervened on Henry's behalf to break the deadlock and persuade the pope to relent. If true, this would have been probably on that third day as the emperor continued to stand barefoot in the winter cold waiting to hear his fate. Gregory might finally have listened to his oldest friend and fellow monk. (It may be no more than a coincidence, but in accordance with Abbot Hugh's rule of justice it became a tradition at Cluny that anyone required to perform public penance was required to stand barefoot at the church door while the congregation sang Mass.)

Lampert concludes his account on an almost domestic note. The pope, he writes, "made a lengthy speech exculpating himself from the charges made by Henry's supporters; he then ate part of the host, and called on the emperor to make a similar oath proclaiming his innocence and good intentions, and to eat the rest. Henry declined; nonetheless, the pope was reasonably well satisfied, concluded his Mass, entertained the emperor to dinner, and sent him on his way."

In trying to assess who came out better, and who worse, from the dramatic events of Canossa, it is ironic that the man whose fortunes most clearly benefited was neither of the two main protagonists. It was Abbot Hugh. After Canossa Pope Gregory engaged Hugh to reform the abbey of Polirone, the principal family monastery of the Countess Matilda. In consequence the influence of Cluny in Italy, especially in Lombardy in the area around Milan, began to grow substantially as Hugh began to receive a veritable flood of gifts of churches, abbeys, and other endowments.

Henry's authority would never be quite the same again after Canossa. He had been compelled to relinquish the ultimate power he cherished; he was no longer the Lord's anointed. For Gregory on the other hand, although apparently the victor at Canossa, events went from bad to worse. Within three years he felt compelled to excommunicate the emperor a second time, and declare him deposed. Henry's response, this time with the support of the German bishops, was to declare the pope himself to be deposed once again, and in June 1080 to appoint the archbishop of Ravenna in his place under the name Clement III. Henry then proceeded to lead an army into Italy, and having first defeated the forces of the formidable Matilda of Tuscany, he marched south and laid siege to Rome, which eventually he captured, concluding his triumph by crowning the new pope in St. Peter's.

There were now two popes in Rome, one of them recognized by the emperor, the other not. Gregory, deposed by Henry and by now humiliated and deserted by most of his cardinals and advisers, took refuge in the Castel Sant'Angelo, a fortress in the heart of the city. And from here, while the siege was in progress, he once more summoned Hugh in the desperate hope that the abbot of Cluny would use his prestige and his influence to negotiate a settlement with the emperor. Hugh, now a man approaching sixty, yet again answered Gregory's plea for help and with a small retinue made his way on horseback from Cluny all the way to a besieged Rome. The emperor had been informed that his godfather was coming, and was waiting in his military headquarters to receive him. But on this occasion Hugh decided to snub him; his sympathies lay with the deposed Gregory—the reformer and fellow monk whom he recognized as the true pope—rather than with his belligerent godson, and accordingly he went straight to the Castel Sant'Angelo. Henry was deeply offended, and though Hugh later agreed to a meeting there was by now no possibility that any attempts at mediation would succeed. Hugh had to turn away from Rome empty-handed, which effectively meant leaving Gregory to his fate. The pope and the abbot never met again.

Isolated in his fortress Gregory appealed for help to one of the most ruthless warlords of the day, the infamous Robert Guiscard, who was the ruler of a large swathe of southern Italy which had been seized by the Normans. Only Gregory's naïveté can have led him to believe that a man such as Guiscard would give a fig for a deposed pope: but an invitation to occupy Rome was quite another matter. Accordingly the Norman warrior duly arrived—in his own time—at the head of a rabble army that without much difficulty seized and plundered the city. The emperor wisely withdrew from Rome at this point, and Guiscard and his men returned south to their Norman lands loaded with loot.

Not surprisingly Gregory now found himself hated by the citizens of Rome, and so, without a title, without supporters, and without a city, he fled south to Salerno, where he died not long afterwards, on May 25, 1085. An early biographer reported his last words: "I have loved justice and hated iniquity. Therefore I die in exile."

Within a few years the first stones of the huge new abbey church at Cluny were being laid. The contrast between this growing spiritual empire in Burgundy and the destruction of the holy city which had always been Cluny's protector would have weighed heavily on Abbot Hugh. He had done everything he could to reconcile the warring factions within Christendom, but could now only look upon the desolation of his plans, for the time being at least. Then, in 1088, after the brief pontificate of Victor III, a new pope was chosen who was to rekindle Hugh's brightest hopes. This was a Frenchman who had himself been trained as a monk at Cluny and was soon to become the abbey's most ardent friend and supporter—Pope Urban II.

VIII.

Rural Peace . . . and Holy War

 Hugh found the strain of these far-flung political commitments increasingly taxing as he grew older. Travel in eleventh-century Europe was scarcely luxurious, and the dramatic confrontations he was forever being drawn into would have taxed the energies of a man half Hugh's age. As someone of profound faith, who was at heart a monk, a private man, even a solitary, he needed a place where he could flee the hectic world—even flee the business of his own monastery—and be alone with his thoughts, and with his God.

A few miles across the low hills to the south of Cluny lies the tiny village of Berzé-la-Ville. And on the crest of a low hill above the village, enclosed by an ancient wall, stands a group of buildings, the most prominent of which is a church tower, squat and plain-looking, and with one of those familiar overhanging roofs that we have come across elsewhere in southern Burgundy. This is the tower of the eleventh-century Chapelle des Moines, which once served a priory so small that it was known simply as a "grange." It belonged to Cluny, and it became the favorite retreat of Abbot Hugh. The chapel itself was almost certainly built under his supervision. An hour's ride on horseback would have taken him there, and it was a journey he made often, whenever he could free himself from monastery affairs.

Landscapes alter far less than towns, and close to the little priory the River Grosne meanders through water meadows just as it would always have done, flanked by graceful willows weighed down by mistletoe, with herons standing sentinel in the shallows, and cattle grazing in lush fields on either side. Just outside the priory walls the Grosne is spanned by a medieval bridge that is only slightly later in date than the one Hugh would have known on the same spot; beyond it the tracks leading out of the valley and up on to the wooded hills are the same timeless paths defined by stone walls that shepherds and farmers have used for centuries.

In springtime these woods are carpeted with white anemones like a million grounded stars. And as the forest gives way to open slopes around Berzé the meadows and orchards are splashed with cowslips. This is truly a lush and pleasant land, and to travel through it makes one understand why in the year 910 Abbot Berno should have announced so unequivocally to Duke William of Aquitaine that here was the region where his lordship's monastery should stand. It is characteristic of the Benedictines that they should have had an instinct for beautiful places in which to worship—God's own country—just as their instinct was for beauty in their litany, their illuminated manuscripts, and in their stone carvings.

The Chapelle des Moines is all that remains of the priory buildings of Hugh's time. The glory of the chapel is the series of richly colored wall paintings, in particular the Christ in Majesty, thirteen feet high, painted early in the twelfth century towards the end of Hugh's life and believed to be an echo of the vast fresco which once dominated the nave of Hugh's new abbey church at Cluny itself. Here at Berzé Christ is depicted handing a parchment to St. Peter calling on him to be the head of the church (a discreet piece of propaganda for the papacy), while at the base of the three windows below are painted representations of the early abbots of the Benedictine Order, including Berno.

What is extraordinary, and deeply sad, is that these rich paintings, strongly Byzantine in influence, are just about the only examples we have of Cluniac church painting from the time of the abbey's glory. And that the paintings even here survive at all is due largely to luck. After the French Revolution the chapel, which was constructed on two levels, became just another storehouse, the lower area being turned into a wine cellar. Then, towards the end of the nineteenth century the priest of Berzé, Abbé Jolivet, visited Hugh's former chapel and was astonished to notice a fragment of a painted head appearing through the flaking distemper of the apse. It transpired that the distemper, whenever it had been applied, had effectively preserved one of the finest examples of Romanesque wall painting in Europe.

Finally, immediately after the Second World War the chapel was bought by the Cluniac scholar Joan Evans, and in 1947 she duly presented it to the Académie de Mâcon. Since then it has been carefully preserved under the watchful eye of the French state.

The Chapelle des Moines is one of the very few places directly associated with Abbot Hugh to have survived. Another, more surprising, survivor stands in the heart of Cluny itself, a stone's throw from the ruins of Hugh's great abbey church. This is the gaunt hunk of a building known as Abbot Hugh's Hostelry, constructed late in the eleventh century at about the time when Hugh was beginning to make his regular escapes to Berzé. Much of the so-called hostelry has been reconstructed over the succeeding centuries, but the massive medieval roof frame survives, as does the stone carving of a lion jutting out from the wall high up under the south gable.

The hostelry was designed for horses, mainly visitors' horses. The sheer size of the place tells us just how many visitors there must have been. Here, then, was where all the lengthy journeys to and from the abbey and all over Europe began and ended. The monks of Cluny bred horses, and they were essential; they were in a sense part of the abbey's lifeblood. Without them Hugh could never have traveled anywhere, no correspondence with kings or emperors or popes could ever have been conducted, and the Cluniac empire, which under Hugh had reached vast proportions, could never have been administered, least of all by just one man—even a man with the extraordinary energies of Abbot Hugh. The horse was his means of command, his invaluable aide.

On March 12, 1088, a man was elected pope who had not only been a monk at Cluny, but had been the abbey's grand prior and thus Hugh's right-hand man: Urban II. Unlike his predecessors he was a Frenchman, born into a noble family just as Hugh had been, and the combination of all these factors made the bond between the two men especially close.

Cluny now had its own man in the Vatican. And the following eleven years, until Urban's death in 1099, represent what was certainly the high point in Hugh's abbacy and indeed in the entire history of the abbey. Cluny had never wielded quite such a dominant influence on the affairs of church and state as it did during these years, and would never do so quite as effectively again. On the very day of his investiture in Rome Urban wrote to Hugh appealing for his prayers and those of his fellow monks. A second letter not long afterwards urged Hugh to come to Rome personally. There followed numerous charters drawn up in favor of Cluny in which the abbey's rights and privileges were confirmed and extended even further than before.

There were sound reasons for the special favors Urban handed out. Seldom had the papacy needed the support of its friends as urgently as it did now. There was still a rival pope in Rome, Clement III, who had been appointed by Emperor Henry IV, and throughout his papacy Urban was to have his work cut out trying to establish himself as the recognized and rightful leader of Western Christianity. He had been one of the few cardinals in Rome loyal to Pope Gregory VII in his final years of exile and humiliation, and in consequence he inherited not only Gregory's reforming zeal, but also his enemies, the emperor in particular, as well as the cardinals and bishops who had supported the antipope. But unlike Gregory, Urban was a natural politician, a character trait he shared with Abbot Hugh.

Urban had a huge, and hugely audacious, ambition, a zealous longing, namely to liberate the city of Jerusalem from "the Infidel." For more than two centuries Christian Europe had appeared weak and helpless in the face of Islam. But now the tide seemed to be turning. Feudal Europe had produced its knights and its warriors. Recent successes in recapturing much of northern Spain from the Moors had planted a new spirit of militant self-confidence among Christian leaders, and an armed Crusade aimed at the conquest of the Holy Land was beginning to seem a practical possibility. Such was Pope Urban's great—and deadly—vision.

It is hardly surprising that he was keen to share this vision with his old friend and former mentor, the abbot of Cluny. Whether Hugh actually shared the pope's call for a holy war against Islam is less certain—his ambitions were rarely spelled out in the open. But Cluny did help Urban win widespread support for the project, both within the church and within the ranks of the feudal nobility, especially in France.

The launching of the First Crusade was the most significant event of Urban's pontificate—indeed it is one of the seminal events of the Middle Ages. And Cluny's contribution to that massive enterprise was, typically of Abbot Hugh, decisive and discreet, but in every way crucial.

Urban's campaign to rally support for the Crusade was conducted with great care and dedication. He first picked his area of operation, which was naturally France, and then proceeded to tour it, spreading the word and making his presence felt. The perfect publicity agency was already at hand—Cluny. In fact there is good reason to believe that the pope's visit to France was actually organized by Cluny.

The pope's ultimate objective in this campaign was to address a grand council of bishops and other high-ranking leaders of the church that he had convoked to be held in the city of Clermont (modern Clermont-Ferrand) in central France during November of 1095. This was to be his platform and his captive audience. Here he would make his appeal; the success of the whole crusading venture would rest on his ability to sway that audience. Meanwhile on the way to Clermont much further work needed to be done: raising funds and troops. And in order to obtain both it was essential to receive the spiritual backing of the most powerful ecclesiastical authority in Europe—Cluny. Without the abbey's support, both moral and material, no plan for a Crusade could possibly come to fruition.

Accordingly, upon arrival in France Urban came first of all to Cluny, with the declared purpose of consecrating Abbot Hugh's partly built new church. Here was an excellent, well-publicized beginning to his goodwill campaign. Then, on a circuitous route to Clermont the pope proceeded to visit a number of Cluny's daughter houses—Marcigny, Souvigny, and Sauxillanges among them—and bestowed on them many of the privileges already granted to Cluny itself. Further goodwill came his way as a result.

By the time Urban reached Clermont his visit was turning into a public relations triumph. Here was a French pope about to preach in France. And Urban took full advantage of the warmth that flowed his way. Among those traveling to Clermont was the seventy-one-year-old Hugh. Much of the council business must have been of marginal interest to him, ecclesiastical matters of a routine nature. But the key moment was to follow. Urban's masterstroke was to conclude the council in the most dramatic way possible—he arranged to make his final address in the open air. A huge crowd duly assembled, and on a cold November morning the pope proceeded to announce his call for a Crusade to the Holy Land. His speech was a tour de force. What the crowd heard, and responded to rapturously, was a measured display of religious fervor in which the goal of liberating Jerusalem was presented as a holy war, a religious as well as a military undertaking, ecclesiastical as well as secular, above all a campaign that would be pleasing to God. From that moment at Clermont the crusading movement was launched.

We know from Cluny's charters of the period that Abbot Hugh proceeded to set about actively encouraging French knights to take part in the pope's great mission. Some historians, notable Hugh Trevor-Roper, have gone so far as to maintain that the Cluniac monasteries actually directed the Crusades. Others have been more cautious, denying that Cluny would have played anything more than a passive role in the military campaigns. But there is no denying the benefits that came Cluny's way as a direct result of the crusading movement. For example, in the year 1096 a nobleman by the name of Achard of Montmerle mortgaged a property in France to Abbot Hugh to pay for an expedition "to Jerusalem in order to fight for God against the pagans and the Saracens." He never returned, and a few years after his death the mortgaged property reverted to Cluny. There are numerous other cases recorded of loans by Cluny to individual adventurers being secured by property. And since the death toll among French Crusaders was alarmingly high, the abbey's ownership of property must have increased considerably as a result. On the other hand, if Crusaders managed to survive and returned home safely then their gratitude towards the monks for their miraculously effective prayers would likewise have meant material benefits.

Other kinds of property came Cluny's way too as a direct result of the First Crusade. Among them were holy relics from the newly conquered Bible lands. In medieval Europe the sanctity and spiritual aura of a church or an abbey was in relation to the importance of the relics in its possession. These were held to possess divine powers, depending on the status of the religious figure from whom they were reputed to come. The closer to the figure of Christ, the more powerful a saint's relics were deemed to be. Spiritual life, and spiritual power, were held to remain after death, and to be vested in surviving evidence of the saint's former presence here on earth. Hence a saint was thought of as dwelling in the church dedicated to him or her, and possession of the relics acted as reassurance of the saint's physical presence there.

The result was a brisk and often cynical trade in fragments of early martyrs or biblical figures, or indeed in any artifacts that could, however loosely, be associated with the life of Christ. Within a few centuries of the supposed discovery of St. James's body in Spain, part of his arm was believed to be in Liège, his hand in Reading and a fragment of his mastoid in Pistoia, besides further relics that were claimed by Toulouse. Chaucer's Pardoner carried with him on his pilgrimage to Canterbury a piece of the sail used by St. Peter on the Sea of Galilee. Another pardoner is reputed to have carried a vial containing the sound of King Solomon's bells.

The cult of holy relics was part of the fabric of medieval Christianity. When one Crusader returned from the Holy Land some years later and gave to Hugh's successor a relic of the martyred St. Stephen, and another presented him with a fragment of the True Cross, both men were offering to Cluny gifts that were incalculably more valuable than gold, or jewels, or castles, or all the rich lands that they had mortgaged in order to wear the cross and play their part in this war.

Urban's great Crusade finally got under way in August of 1096. One of the contingents was led by Hugh of Vermondois, brother of King Philip I of France. A second contingent was led by a Norman from southern Italy, Bohemond, son of the infamous Robert Guiscard who had answered Pope Gregory's desperate appeal for help in Rome by sacking the city. A third army was led by the grizzled warrior Raymond of Saint-Gilles, Count of Toulouse, accompanied by the bishop of Le Puy. And the fourth army was under the command of Robert II of Flanders.

The First Crusade was a grandiloquent and grisly feudal exercise in which chivalry somewhat unexpectedly came of age. An estimated four thousand mounted knights took part, supported by at least twenty-five thousand infantry. The campaign ground on for almost three years until Jerusalem finally fell to the Crusader armies in July of 1099.

Pope Urban never lived to enjoy what would have been his greatest triumph; he died just a few weeks before the capture of the Holy City. Within a year there was a Christian king in Jerusalem and a colony of Cluniac monks firmly established. Hugh's expanded empire now embraced the very birthplace of Christianity.

IX.

Looking towards England

 The transition of Normandy from piracy to piety was swift and surprising. At the beginning of the tenth century much of France was still being subjected to the "Norman fury." Nowhere felt safe from marauding bands of these Scandinavian pirates. Towns, villages, churches, farms, and crops were repeatedly devastated by them. Yet within little more than half a century the duke of Normandy, Richard I, was appealing to Abbot Mayeul of Cluny for monks to be sent to a Christian community he had established at the coastal town of Fécamp. The conversion of Normandy to Christianity must have seemed to its neighbors little short of miraculous.

Mayeul had cautiously declined Duke Richard's appeal, perhaps suspicious of risking his charges in a territory that not so long ago had been the domain of brigands. Then early in the eleventh century the duke's successor, Richard II, was able to persuade the most influential churchman of the day, the Italian-Burgundian monk William of Volpiano, to come to Fécamp and introduce Cluniac discipline to the new abbey. William's impact on Normandy was huge—before long there was a burgeoning of monastic life in the young dukedom. After Fécamp a number of great abbeys were founded, among them Jumièges, Mont-St.-Michel, St.-Ouen, Bernay, Caen, Bec-Hellouin, and St.-Wandrille, until Normandy rapidly became among the most respected centers of learning in Europe, as well as of architecture, sculpture, painting, and music. The Italian Benedictine Lanfranc was attracted to the new monastery of Bec where he became prior before being appointed the first abbot of St. Stephen's at Caen (and ultimately Archbishop of Canterbury). Another distinguished Italian scholar, Anselm, followed Lanfranc to Bec, where he became abbot before eventually succeeding Lanfranc as head of the church in England (in which capacity he made a special visit to Cluny in order to renew his relationship with Abbot Hugh).

Without the Cluniac ideals of monastic reform as a driving force few of these achievements would have been likely. As it was, the impact of Cluny had in a very short time made itself felt in the newest and most energetic Christian territory in Europe. And from here, since the dukes of Normandy harbored ambitions far beyond their small land, that impact would very soon be carried northwards across the Channel. The most famous date in English history, 1066, also signaled the beginning of Cluniac influence there.

Hugh had been abbot of Cluny for seventeen years at the time of the Norman Conquest of England. And during those seventeen years Cluny had been the dominant influence on monastic affairs in Normandy. But the relationship between the lord of Cluny and the new king of England is hard to fathom. They were hardly close. There is only one record of the two men having actually met, and that was not until a good many years after the Conquest. The account comes from one of Hugh's more fanciful biographers, Gilo, a man generally concerned with his subject's saintliness rather than with the truth. Gilo almost certainly never met Hugh, and wrote his account of the abbot's life in Rome more than a decade after Hugh's death, and at the request of his successor. However, true or false, Gilo claimed that a meeting took place in Normandy, at which the king of England paid Hugh "such honor and gave him such gifts that no one in this life could have believed it possible." These gifts included his cloak—his "coppa"—the surface of which shone with gold, amber, and pearls, and carried a row of golden bells at the base. At this point, Gilo continues, William bowed his head "as if an angel from heaven had offered him divine grace."

Even allowing for hagiographical excess the Conqueror clearly regarded Hugh with considerable reverence. Hugh on the other hand seems to have treated William with rather less than awe—almost in fact as an inferior. It may simply be that Hugh, who had shown himself to be an exceptionally shrewd judge of character, recognized in William a man who was even more of a supreme controller than he was himself, and was therefore determined not to be put in the position of being required to hand over authority in monastic matters to the new ruler of England.

This note of suspicion on Hugh's part became especially noticeable in his reaction to King William's repeated request for Cluniac monks to be sent to England. For once Hugh seems to have been a reluctant evangelist. In fact Cluny's links with England came about in an almost accidental way—by proxy. The intermediary was one of the Conqueror's most trusted supporters among the new Norman rulers of England, by the name of William de Warenne, a man of learning and of deep piety. On the advice of the new archbishop of Canterbury, Lanfranc, Warenne agreed to restore the ancient priory of St. Pancras, in Lewes, rebuilding it "of wood and stone," with the intention of establishing it as the first Cluniac foundation in England. He also proceeded to make a gift to the church of "land for six plows."

Accompanied by his wife, Warenne then set off on a pilgrimage to Rome. But as a result of various hindrances along the way the two travelers decided to make for Cluny instead. As unofficial ambassadors of the king of England they were treated with the warmest hospitality, and so impressed were they with everything they found during their prolonged stay at the abbey that they decided to make a request that monks from Cluny be sent to England to the priory at Lewes, now in the process of being restored. No decision could be made without the agreement of Hugh who was absent from the abbey at the time, doubtless on one of his prolonged tours of Cluny's numerous dependencies. Nevertheless, Warenne managed to get a letter to him asking for three or four monks. Hugh was reluctant at first, but on his return to Cluny he met Warenne and was eventually persuaded to send four monks to England.

Hugh seems to have been impressed by William de Warenne—more so possibly than he was by William the Conqueror—since he also gave his promise that Cluny would always appoint as prior of Lewes the holiest monk available after the grand prior of Cluny himself. Warenne also fixed the tax to be paid to Cluny on behalf of Lewes at fifty English "solidi" a year.

William himself wrote to Hugh a number of times begging him to send further monks to Lewes. In all fairness, Hugh's reluctance was understandable, since there were simply not enough Cluniac monks to go round. And, as Hugh explained privately, England was "a foreign land far distant by sea." He was not prepared to say as much to William directly, preferring to prevaricate. A letter to the Conqueror dated 1078 survives, managing to say "No" in highly circuitous language, and which we know aroused William to anger—he was not a man accustomed to being denied. In response William resorted to a refined form of bribery, offering Hugh the sum of one hundred silver pounds a year for each monk Cluny would be prepared to send. Hugh refused again, stating that any such agreement would be both undignified and unchristian—a somewhat flawed argument considering the handsome flow of funds regularly being poured into Cluny's coffers from its religious houses across Europe, as well as the revenues from more than one hundred separate properties, not to mention the huge annual payments from King Alfonso of Spain.

Altogether Hugh seems at his least impressive when dealing with the new king of England—there is little of the charm and courtesy that he regularly displayed towards other rulers as well as to successive occupants of the papacy.

It is unclear just how many monks from Cluny did eventually arrive at Lewes; certainly there were not as many as the Conqueror hoped, though there must have been enough to create a surge of Cluniac activity in England during the decades following the Norman Conquest. The motherhouse of the English Cluniacs remained Lewes, though before long further foundations came into existence as the result of extensive gifts of land, at least five of them receiving the same privileges as Cluny itself, and becoming known as the "daughters of Cluny." They included, besides Lewes in 1077, Wenlock in about 1080, Bermondsey in 1082, Castle Acre in 1089, Pontefract in about 1090, and Thetford in 1104. By the end of Hugh's abbacy there were no fewer than thirty-six Cluniac houses in England, many of them dependencies of other English priories, and of which at least twelve were by now fully organized monasteries.

The abbey was growing inordinately wealthy. Everything Cluny touched made it richer yet. The First Crusade increased its revenues conspicuously. Then there were the more regular payments from abroad, far and away the largest being the annual tribute by King Alfonso; in addition, all subject houses in Italy, Spain, and France were expected to make an annual contribution to Cluny.

In the meanwhile local benefits were also mounting. One of the many privileges Cluny enjoyed was to be exempt from tolls. Monks and lay brothers, as well as visitors of all kinds, ecclesiastical or otherwise, could come and go at will. It was like having a diplomatic passport. The abbey was also permitted to mint its own coins. In Abbot Hugh's time money tended to be regarded not so much as a currency but as a commodity best converted into precious and beautiful objects designed to adorn the new abbey church. Money certainly was not something to be hoarded—it merely facilitated the acquisition of rich and splendid things which spoke of the glories of heaven, nothing being considered too lavish or rare for the service of God.

Predictably, this was not how Cluny's critics were apt to regard the abbey's taste for luxury. Charges of vanity and personal aggrandizement were already rumbling in the eleventh century, though these were but small warnings of what was to come in the centuries to follow. It was probably no more than an expression of gratitude, or of personal admiration, that led Pope Urban to bestow on Hugh the right to wear pontifical vestments at Mass—consisting of purple gloves, a jeweled miter and gold-embroidered shoes. There is no record of Hugh actually availing himself of these sumptuous vanities (it would have been contrary to his nature) although there can be no doubt that many of his successors did so with full pomp and self-esteem.

Cluny's greatest wealth, though, lay in the possession of land in huge quantities, the result of a flood of donations by wealthy laymen. Novices, many of whom came from rich feudal families, would also bring gifts of land with them. The Cluniac scholar

Noreen Hunt has stated that "the accumulation of so much property by a single establishment is phenomenal." The monks had become landlords on a vast scale. It is recorded that under Hugh the abbey came to own over a hundred different territories, many of them locally in the Mâconnais area, and these included woods, pastures, fields, salt deposits, quarries, as well as vineyards and what were described as "grain lands."

The very phrase "grain lands" points to a further development which worked in Cluny's favor. Western Europe was enjoying what amounted to a revolution in farming. Earlier in the Middle Ages feuding warlords and foreign marauders had come close to paralyzing rural life and rural economy. However, by the mid-eleventh century the restoration of some degree of political and social order was resulting in a widespread growth in population, coinciding with an increase in prosperity, which in turn was leading to large areas of unused land being cleared and put to the plow. Farming methods themselves were becoming more efficient; instead of the ineffective wooden spike which did little more than scratch the surface of a field, farmers were beginning to use the iron plowshare, of German origin, which was drawn by oxen and which turned the soil over more deeply and much more effectively. The result was greatly increased productivity of the land, and this in turn made crop rotation possible, as well as certain fields being allowed to rest each year rather than becoming exhausted through overcultivation.

More territory, too, became available for stock breeding, particularly of horses, which were essential to the economy of Cluny as well as being the best means of transport. As we have seen, the numerous and lengthy journeys which the administration of Cluny's empire required of Abbot Hugh and his monastic staff would have been impossible without a large stock of horses permanently available.

The increasing wealth of the land meant not only the increasing wealth of Cluny; it spilt over into the town which had sprung up round the abbey and which in a sense serviced it. The burg of Cluny now had proper roads linking it to the outside world, and whereas originally its inhabitants had been merely servants and peasants working for the abbey, before long there grew up an independent class of prosperous traders, craftsmen, and entrepreneurs who fed successfully on the prestige and fame of the most powerful religious house in Europe. It is no accident that Cluny today, small town though it is, still possesses some of the most strikingly handsome Romanesque houses to be found anywhere on the continent. They are dwellings that speak of considerable prosperity.

Not surprisingly, the combination of riches and privileges enjoyed by Cluny often aroused profound hostility both among

sections of the local feudal society and the church authorities. One particular source of enmity was the hilltop town of Brancion, in the heart of the Mâconnais some fifteen miles northeast of Cluny near the great Lombard abbey church of Tournus. The lords of Brancion were a constant thorn in Cluny's side, venting their fury at its growing power and prestige by repeatedly plundering its lands, seizing its cattle, and on more than one occasion actually attacking the abbey itself. There was a certain absurdity in these aggressive outbursts, because each act of lawlessness would result in a complaint by the abbot to no less an authority than the pope himself, in consequence of which the lords of Brancion repeatedly found themselves excommunicated. Abject displays of remorse would follow, accompanied by healthy donations to the abbey's coffers and, on at least one occasion, a commitment to participate in a Crusade to the Holy Land. Penance thus duly enacted, and the papal punishment lifted, the bellicose lords would promptly resume their pillaging and cattle theft until the next sentence of excommunication was issued by Rome. And so it went on.

Abbot Hugh's patience was even more severely tested by the hostility of certain local bishops, especially the bishop of Mâcon. The dispute invariably came down to a matter of money and what the bishop felt to be an erosion of his personal authority; because Cluny now owned so many churches in the Mâconnais, revenues that would originally have been paid to the bishopric were no longer being received. In addition the bishop did not have any say in the administration of these churches and their parishes.

Matters had come to a head some years earlier, in 1079, when the bishop won the backing of the archbishop of Lyon. The latter proceeded to take himself to Rome in order to plead the bishop's case with the then pope, Gregory VII. However, the pope's strong personal links with Abbot Hugh gave the archbishop small chance of a sympathetic hearing. The only concession Gregory made was to send a legate to Burgundy to try to resolve the dispute amicably. Alas, the mood in Mâcon was far from amicable, and the hapless legate by the name of Warmund was physically attacked and stripped of his pontifical regalia, the final act in the drama being that the bishop himself was stripped of his office and all those implicated in the assault were excommunicated.

Pope Gregory's personal verdict on the incident, imparted to one of his aides, was that the bishop had been a simple dove faced with the cunning of a serpent in the figure of Abbot Hugh—an interesting observation from a man who knew the abbot well. Hugh generally seems too diplomatic a figure to allow a quality like "cunning" to show in his complex dealings with rulers and churchmen. But clearly Gregory saw a different man.

The abbey's lands have long ago been confiscated and dispersed, those that survived until the eighteenth century being finally swept away on the floodtide of anticlerical feeling which accompanied the French Revolution. Yet there is at least one surprising exception. A few miles northeast of Cluny, not far from where the lords of Brancion once launched their raids on the abbey's property, is the vine-growing village of Cruzille. It may not be as famous as its neighboring village Chardonnay, but it has a special significance within the story of Cluny. One of the principal estates about a mile outside the village is entitled Domaine des Vignes du Maynes, inscribed in bold lettering on the side of a sprawling Burgundian farmhouse.

The estate is owned today by a vigneron by the name of Alain Guillot, whose family has lived in the village for many generations, and who now runs it with his son on organic principles. But Monsieur Guillot also operates the place as a small museum. He points out that the massive stone wall which flanks one of the huge storage areas dates from Romano-Gallic times. Close by stands a pictorial "family tree" of the estate, described as a *Genéalogie des Vignes du Maynes*. This traces the ownership of the vineyard back through the centuries until, at the base of the tree, are inscribed the words *Abbaye de Cluny*.

Nearby, resting against the wall, is the prize exhibit of Monsieur Guillot's little museum. This is a *borne*, or boundary stone, some three feet in height, near the top of which is engraved the coat of arms of the abbey, the crossed keys and sword of St. Peter and St. Paul.

The *borne* was found on the edge of one of the vineyards by Guillot's father, and has been dated to the middle of the twelfth century, no more than a few decades after Hugh was abbot, though it is conceivable that Cluny's ownership of these lands may have gone back earlier than this—Les Vignes du *Maynes*, the name of the vineyard since the sixteenth century, was originally Les Vignes des *Moynes*—the Monks' Vines. In other words the monks of Cluny may have enjoyed the delicious wines of Cruzille for more than six hundred years.

Indeed, St. Benedict in his Rule recommended a daily ration of wine for his monks. For all the severity of their monastic life—or perhaps precisely because of it—consumption of wine, in moderation, was never among the prohibitions they were expected to endure. A hallowed tradition grew out of such humane leniency—monks became among the first apothecaries and the first distillers. Benedictine and Chartreuse are merely two of the better-known liqueurs to have originated in the laboratories of monasteries. There are scores of others throughout much of Europe.

It is a heartening thought that Abbot Hugh may have enjoyed a daily tumbler of Mâcon-Villages throughout his sixty years in office.

X.

The Greatest Church in Christendom

It is a fair assumption that nothing in Abbot Hugh's long life—neither the Crusades, nor the reconquest of Spain, nor dealings with popes and emperors, kings and princes, not even his own vast empire—meant as much to him as Cluny's new abbey church.

One of Hugh's less fanciful biographers wrote of the church that "it took twenty years to build, was so spacious that thousands of monks could assemble there, so magnificent that an emperor could have built nothing finer, and that it surpassed all known churches in construction and beauty."

It was an assessment very close to the truth. To have built something quite so ambitious, so far ahead of its time, was remarkable enough. To have done so relatively quickly was nothing less than astonishing, even though in fact it did take rather longer than the twenty years Hugh's biographer claimed. The first stones were laid in 1088. By October 1095, when Pope Urban II came to consecrate the high altar, the whole east end of the church was complete with its broad semicircle of an ambulatory and five radial chapels. Five years later the two transepts were ready, and by 1115 the entire west front had been built. The nave—about 250 feet in length—had been vaulted by the year 1121, one year after Hugh had been canonized by Pope Calixtus II (the abbot having died twelve years earlier).

Four years later disaster struck. The roof of the nave collapsed— a not uncommon occurrence in church construction at the time. Nonetheless, it was swiftly rebuilt, this time securely, and the final dedication of the great basilica by Pope Innocent II took place on October 25, 1130, just forty-two years after those first stones had been laid.

It was far and away the largest and greatest church ever built— a true wonder of the world. It had been entirely Abbot Hugh's conception, and his lifelong dream. According to a Cluniac text of the period, Abbot Hugh, "encouraged by a message from on high, built a basilica like a tent for the glory of God . . . of such splendor that if the inhabitants from heaven could content themselves with our terrestrial dwellings, one would say that here was the angels' 'courtyard.' "

How much of the actual design was due to Hugh himself is impossible to tell. The architect of the new church was said to be an elderly monk by the name of Gunzo, who was the retired abbot of Cluny's parent house of Baume-les-Messieurs. But apart from being a man of very advanced years Gunzo was known principally as a musician, and although the requirements of the liturgy would have been a major consideration in the design of the abbey church it is hard to imagine such a man playing a major role in so vast and complex an architectural project. The more likely candidate was a younger monk whom we know to have been Gunzo's collaborator, by the name of Hezelon of Liège; the fact that he was a mathematician makes his role as the leading architect even more likely. But since this is all we know about the man, the ultimate responsibility for one of the supreme architectural achievements in Christian Europe will remain forever a question mark.

The new abbey church, labeled Cluny III by modern historians, was enormous. Abbot Hugh had insisted on a church that could accommodate all Cluniac monks should they ever be brought together. It was to be the all-embracing, all-protecting mother of the entire order. And in this way it symbolized Hugh's own position as the supreme and sole authority in the Cluniac empire. The church measured a total of over 580 feet in length. Its height was even more impressive considering the relatively primitive system of hoists and pulleys available to the medieval masons: a breathtaking one hundred feet from floor to roof.

The only way this vertiginous height can be experienced today is by standing within the one surviving south transept, and gazing far upwards towards the roof and the glorious octagon bell tower that today is Cluny's most famous landmark, the Clocher de l'Eau Bénite, the Holy Water Belfry. The imagination then has to multiply that experience to embrace the nine-tenths of the church that is no longer there.

That we know more or less exactly the structure and proportions of Hugh's great church is due in part to the existence of a number of drawings and lithographs made by traveling artists in the eighteenth century in search of picturesque rural scenes to sell back in Paris, unaware of course that within a few years their charming efforts would be virtually the only surviving evidence of this great church. In recent times a further contribution to our knowledge has come from computer graphics. The information which has been fed into computers in order to create a visual reconstruction of the church comes from two sources: firstly, careful measurements made on the ground, and secondly, reconstructive drawings of the church made by the American archaeologist Kenneth John Conant after many years of meticulous research at Cluny before and after the Second World War.

As a result we know today that Cluny III was a five-aisled basilica, with two side aisles running down both sides of the broad nave. There was not just one, but two transepts, further contributing to what must have been a bewildering forest of perspectives. As befitted a pilgrim church, a semicircular ambulatory with five radial chapels allowed worshipers to progress behind the high altar in order to admire the holy relics that would have been placed upon it on special feast days. Above the altar and the ambulatory the huge dome of the apse contained a fresco which centered on an image of Christ in Majesty at least double life-size. A surviving lithograph from the eighteenth century shows nothing clearly beyond this central figure, though we know from a description of the painting written down shortly before its destruction in 1798 that Christ was surrounded by the symbols of the four evangelists, accompanied by the twenty-four old men of the Apocalypse and a choir of angels.

The nave itself had eleven bays, above each of which rose two arcades of rounded arches. The two arms of the larger transept were both surmounted by towers, the southern arm by the Clocher de l'Eau Bénite, and the northern arm by the Clocher des Bisans (where a set of bells came to be hung that were cast in England and presented to the abbey later in the twelfth century by Matilda, the granddaughter of William the Conqueror). The largest of the towers, the Clocher du Choeur, rose in the center of the church, above the main crossing, where the larger transept crossed the nave; another smaller tower, the Clocher des Lampes, rose immediately to the east of it, where the smaller transept intersected the nave. (Two further towers at the western end of the church, the Barabans, were added at a later date, so completing the effect of a gigantic architectural mountain.)

Almost as grave as the loss of the huge fresco is that of nearly all the carved capitals, apart from the few that are preserved in the two local museums, the Musée du Farinier and the Musée d'Art et d'Archéologie. There has been wide disagreement about the exact number of capitals Cluny III would have contained. It has been claimed that there might have been at least a thousand, but even the most conservative figure of five hundred still points to a massive loss of what were certainly among the earliest Romanesque carvings in France.

Just how early the surviving capitals are likely to have been remains disputed among Cluniac scholars. We know that the high altar and the chancel were consecrated by Pope Urban II in 1095. If the delicately carved capitals now preserved in the Musée du Farinier were already in place at that time, then they are thought to represent a degree of artistic sophistication considerably ahead of their time. And for this reason more skeptical voices have insisted that the capitals must be at least twenty years later.

Probably the gravest loss of all is the carved tympanum that once dominated the main portal at the western end. The entire portal was planned under Hugh, though in all probability carried out later, during the second decade of the twelfth century. We know in the broadest terms what the great tympanum would have looked like. Christ in Glory was invariably the dominant theme of Cluniac carvings on the exterior of church entrances, examples of which survive in southern Burgundy on churches built under the inspiration of Cluny—Charlieu, Mont-St.-Vincent, and Anzy-le-Duc being among the best of them. Conant's reconstruction drawings of the Cluny tympanum make it clear that the central figure of Christ was supported by angels and flanked by the usual symbols of Matthew, Mark, Luke, and John, while on the lintel below was the figure of the Virgin Mary accompanied by the customary twenty-four elders of the Apocalypse, all of them gazing upwards towards Christ.

We may understand the iconography of the lost Cluny tympanum, but alas we can have no sense at all of its artistic grandeur—its beauty, its skill, how it might compare with some of the great church portals in Burgundy which undoubtedly owed so much to it, directly or indirectly, notably those of Vézelay and Autun.

A smaller version of Cluny III does exist. The Basilique du Sacré-Coeur at Paray-le-Monial stands beside a tributary of the Loire some twenty-five miles to the west of Cluny, on the edge of the Brionnais region, that southernmost area of Burgundy between the River Loire to the west and the wooded hills of the Beaujolais to the east and south. Here Abbot Hugh's family were the local lords, and it was at the instigation of Hugh that Sacré-Coeur was built, taking the abbey church as its model. Paray had been one of Cluny's earliest dependent priories, dating from the 970s when Abbot Mayeul was offered the land by the local count on the advice of his son, the bishop of Auxerre, a man later to become Hugh's great-uncle.

Like many imitations, particularly those of smaller scale, Paray misses both the grandeur and (one suspects) the artistry of the original. Much of it feels like a pastiche, plain and soulless in a way that Cluny III most certainly never was. Yet the octagon bell tower is as fine as the one surviving at Cluny, and the most intriguing feature of the church is the sculpture surrounding the door of the south transept. Unlike other Cluniac portals the carving here is entirely abstract. There are no angels, no demons, no figures representing Lust, no twenty-four elders of the Apocalypse; instead there are just intricate geometrical patterns—chevrons, squares, diamond shapes, stars, entwined knots. This area of the basilica was consecrated in the year 1104, just five years before the death of the church's progenitor. But at the time when Paray was being planned Hugh was making his second and last visit to Spain to meet Cluny's most generous patron, King Alfonso VI. Here is an appropriate occasion for speculation. It seems very likely that during his prolonged stay in Spain the delicacy of Moorish geometrical carving, both on mosques and on a variety of domestic buildings, would have made an impression on Hugh, because he would have seen it everywhere. Maybe it struck him that such wonderfully sophisticated rhythms in stone might actually be more capable of drawing human thoughts towards the contemplation of heaven than the explicit representations of good and evil being coming from the masons' yards of Christian Europe. In a society that was already beginning to learn so much from Islam—in science, in mathematics, in medicine, and in philosophy—here was another debt to the Moors.

Cluny's own building program, if it may be called that, reached its apogee in the last two decades of Hugh's abbacy and in the two decades that followed. The reason is not hard to find: these were the years of Cluny's greatest wealth, and by far the largest proportion of the abbey's vast income went into the construction of new religious houses, priories, hostels and, above all, churches. Raoul Glaber's "white mantle of churches" would have seemed to him even more magnificent and all-embracing had he lived one hundred years later. "The concentration of resources on such buildings as these has astonished many modern observers," writes the medievalist Christopher Brooke. "Some have condemned them as wasteful, since they meant spending on stone, paint and reliquaries money that might have gone to feed the poor; others have been the more impressed by the dedication of funds and skills to a sacred cause."

This explosion of church building of necessity meant a proliferation of masons' yards and craftsmen's workshops. The days of the itinerant Lombards moving from place to place, leaving their distinctive mark on everything they built, were long gone. Now workshops were springing up all over the place, dictated by demand. The Cluniac patrons and paymasters were happy to take advantage of whatever local talent was available, and in addition masons and master carvers now headed for Burgundy from any number of different regions, either to work on the great abbey church itself or on one of the smaller churches being built in the towns and villages of the Mâconnais and Brionnais regions.

As a result there is little consistency of style, or of quality, about the carvings decorating the new Burgundian churches. It is hard to define the "art of Cluny" since Cluniac sculpture varies so widely from church to church—between the lyrical and the phantasmagoric, the stiff and the fluid, the sophisticated and the primitive. At its finest there is a warm humanist spirit about Cluniac stone carving, a feeling of sensuous joy at the living world, and nowhere is this more strongly evident than in those ambulatory capitals from the abbey church now preserved at the Musée du Farinier—both those representing the eight tones of the Gregorian chant, and the ones illustrating the seasons. "Spring," for example, is represented by the graceful figure of a girl in secular clothes which seem to flutter around her, accompanied by the inscription "Spring brings the first flowers, and the first scents."

Characteristic of the best Cluniac sculpture is an elegant, even sensuous elongation of the human form. This is visible in the portals of several churches in the region, and is finally brought to a triumphant level a few decades later by the sculptors who were responsible for two of the outstanding creative achievements of the Middle Ages, the carved portals at Autun and Vézelay (see chapter 17).

But if anywhere may be said to be the true homeland of Cluniac architecture and sculpture, apart from Cluny itself, then we need to look no further than the Brionnais, Abbot Hugh's homeland. Almost every village here possesses a small Romanesque church, mostly built of a warm gold-tinted sandstone which makes them appear to glow in the evening light, especially those like Châteauneuf and Montceaux-l'Etoile which are set in open land as though the better to be admired.

This is a land of little streams and small farms, each territory divided up by an intricate latticework of hedges. It is also cattle country; the principal town in the region is Charolles, which has given its name to the breed of white cattle, the Charolais, now bred for beef all over France. The church of St.-Julien-de-Jonzy even possesses a carved capital depicting the head of a cow, as if asking for God's blessing on the local industry.

Signposts in the region offer a *Circuit des Églises Romanes,* though in fact almost any direction will serve just as well. Heading south from Paray-le-Monial the first village is Montceaux-l'Etoile. The church, built of a striking blend of red and yellow sandstone, possesses one of the most beautiful Cluniac portals in the Brionnais, on the theme of the Ascension of Christ—in common with a great many of the churches in the region. Barely a mile further south is another of the gems of the Brionnais, Anzy-le-Duc, with its handsome Cluniac portal, again on the theme of the Ascension, and a three-story octagonal bell tower that rises like a lighthouse above the flat landscape.

Following the river line southwards we pass Marcigny, where the first Cluniac nunnery (no longer surviving) was founded by Abbot Hugh, before heading eastwards past Semur-en-Brionnais with its grim castle where Hugh was born. A mile or so further on we reach St.-Julien-de-Jonzy, which boasts a striking Cluniac church with a tympanum of Christ in Glory above a particularly fine lintel depicting the Last Supper, the entire ensemble carved from a single block of stone.

Our *Circuit* could then take us northwards to Varenne-l'Arconce, another handsome church quite out of scale with the tiny village in which it is set, or eastwards to Châteauneuf with its tower like an index finger pointing to heaven, or northwest to Bois-Sainte-Marie with its majestic façade and nave capitals that are carved with horrific beasts and demons administering a variety of fairly basic tortures on hapless sinners.

If there is to be an appropriate finale, then let it be the town of Charlieu that lies just beyond the borders of the Brionnais to the south. Here are the ruins of one of the earliest Benedictine abbeys in France, which later became a dependency of Cluny. The abbey church itself is likewise mostly ruined, except for a fine cloister arcade and, in particular, a narthex and north doorway that contain some of the finest twelfth-century Cluniac carvings to be found in the whole region. The tympanum here shows a typical Brionnais stylization of the Ascension, Christ in Majesty framed by two angels and the symbols of the four evangelists. On the lintel below, the Virgin Mary is attended by two angels and surrounded by the twelve apostles. One of the accompanying capitals depicts the figure of Lust, represented here by a woman being devoured by snakes and toads—lust was the favorite sin of a misogynist church.

Our view of what constitutes the art of Cluny is to a great extent distorted by accidents of history. We tend to concentrate on sculpture and architecture since by and large these are what have survived, even if the motherhouse has not. In fact, the abbey itself played little creative part in either of these activities; monks were neither carvers nor masons. The two artistic skills that the monks of Cluny actually practiced were book illumination and music.

The Cluniac liturgy was the pride of the monastery, and singing seems to have gone on in the abbey church for much of every day and night. Visiting popes and other church and civic dignitaries frequently commented on it with awe. From the earliest days under Abbot Odo music was always considered at Cluny to be something sacred, a projection of a divine spirituality capable of reaching the souls of those who practised it as well as those who listened—hence its importance in the daily liturgy. No names of individual musicians or composers remain, but handwritten pages of musical notation in plainsong (or "plainchant") have survived from Cluny dating from as early as the eleventh century, suggesting that there would always have been skilled musical practitioners among the monks.

As for book illustration, we know that the abbey's scriptorium was a hallowed place, and that a team of monks was responsible for some of the most glorious work of illumination in medieval Europe: Bibles, Gospels, bestiaries, psalters, commentaries on the Apocalypse, lectionaries, books of offices, antiphonals, lives of the saints. But here history has delivered a lethal blow. Much of the great library at Cluny was destroyed by the Huguenots during the Wars of Religion in 1562, and most of what managed to survive that conflagration then perished at the hands of the French Revolutionary mobs in the late eighteenth century. The Bibliothèque Nationale in Paris preserves most of what little remains, just enough to point to the magnitude of what has perished.

Cluniac wall painting, too, is a rarity. The finest example which has survived is the large fresco of Christ in Majesty in the apse of the Chapelle des Moines at the former grange, or priory, of Berzé-la-Ville, Abbot Hugh's favorite retreat.

Hugh was now well into his eighties; how much time he spent at Berzé in his last years we can only surmise. But the place soon became something of a shrine preserved in his memory. In the year of his death, 1109, three monks named Seguius, Fulcherius, and Glocens undertook to restore the entire priory, probably in the great man's honor.

It was on Maundy Thursday, 1109, that Hugh presided over the chapter reading as usual, and then supervised the distribution of food to the poor. (It is on record that in a single year two hundred and fifty hams were distributed at Cluny, fifty people were fed daily with bread and wine, and alms given to seventeen thousand poor.) Then on Easter Day he entered the abbey church clothed all in white and joined in a chanting procession. That evening eye-witnesses noticed that his strength seemed to be failing, and the following day he was clearly much weaker. "His radiant eyes grew dim," it was reported, "his tongue heavy, his chest twitched, his knees trembled, and his face grew white." He still lingered four more days. Finally he asked to be lifted up and laid on a bed of ashes and cinders before the altar in the Lady Chapel which he had built. And there, stretched out on that bed of ashes, he died.

Hugh's principal legacy is something that no longer exists—the great abbey church which Christopher Brooke has described as "the supreme expression of scale, proportion, decoration, wealth of ornament, richness of liturgy and music, in the Europe of the early twelfth century."

What he also bequeathed was a Cluniac empire that now stretched across the continent of Europe and beyond, as far as the Levant. By Hugh's death there were Cluniac monasteries throughout France, as well as in England, Spain, Italy, Switzerland, Germany, and what is now Belgium. In total there were some 1,450 monasteries and 10,000 monks. It was an empire that had made Cluny the spiritual heart of Europe, with Hugh himself as its spiritual ruler. His personal authority had been total and unquestioned. One measure of that absolute rule was Hugh's insistence that all novices had to be admitted to the order at Cluny, and only at Cluny; furthermore every monk, however far away he might reside, was required to visit the motherhouse at least once in his lifetime. This was not simply Hugh's insistence on keeping an eye on everything—it was his belief that Cluny possessed a spiritual quality that acted as a kind of blessing on all those who could bring themselves to visit the place.

Hugh's insistence on personal control, however benevolent this might be, inevitably invited problems, particularly as he grew older and was less able to travel. His unwillingness to delegate to sub-ordinates meant that there was never any clear chain of command running through the Cluniac order. Everything depended on the abbot's word. His was a benign dictatorship. This absence of structure also meant an increasing lack of close contact with the political world outside the order, and hence an increasing lack of awareness of political events that had a direct bearing on the abbey, particularly on its finances. By the time of Hugh's death Cluny's income, though still huge, was beginning to fall, largely because gifts to the abbey, once so lavish, were now tailing off. These were as yet small storm clouds gathering over the abbey, but in the decades to come they were to build into threatening proportions.

For a while the news of Hugh's death created a sense of hiatus at Cluny. The institution felt an emptiness, a general numbness, amounting to a feeling of bewilderment, even disbelief. It was said by those at the abbey that there was hardly anyone who could remember a time when Hugh was *not* the abbot of Cluny.

XI

Daily Life at Cluny

The long decades of Hugh's reign saw Cluny grow into a world of its own. Daily life within those massive walls became meticulously ordered, almost metronomic in its precision, and largely inward-looking as if deliberately turning its back on the vastness of the empire of which it was actually the hub. It was a secret world within a world. But archaeological research over the past fifty years has uncovered some of those secrets, enabling us to reconstruct the elaborate layout of the place.

To the north of the elaborate complex of buildings stood the abbey church itself, Cluny III. Immediately to the south of the church was the abbot's personal chapel. This opened on to the great cloister (*claustrum*) where the monks would spend much of their time between services working, reading, and—when it was permitted—talking to each other. On the edge of the cloister stood a fountain where the monks would wash their hands before meals in the refectory (*refectorium*) which was immediately beyond it.

Along the west side of the cloister was a range of smaller buildings. Nearest to the refectory was the bakery, and next to it a kitchen (*coquina*), one of several. Close by was a second kitchen for the use of the lay brothers. These were members of the community who had not taken monastic vows, and whose daily life was for the most part separate from that of the monks—increasingly so as the day-to-day timetable of a monk's life became more and more ritualized. The role of the lay brothers at Cluny therefore changed, becoming ever more central to the efficient running of the place as they came to take on nearly all the required physical tasks, from cooking and baking to washing up, from gardening to maintaining the wine cellar, from keeping the fish ponds and beehives to grooming the horses, even attending to the general maintenance of the abbey—in fact virtually everything that was not to do with prayers, singing, or copying and decorating manuscripts.

Near the kitchens were the abbey's workshops and the *scriptorium*, and large storehouses for grain, oil, and vegetables brought from the extensive garden that was located to the north of the church. Also to the west were the lay brothers' and servants' living quarters as well as the abbey's stables, and the accommodations for visitors (*hospitium*). Guest houses tended to be conveniently close to the church so that visitors could join in the services if they wished without having to intrude on the daily routine of the monks. The monks' dormitory (*dormitorium*) was on the east side of the cloister, on the first floor above the chapter house, the *capitulum*.

Further to the east still was the infirmary (*infirmaria*), equipped with its own chapel for those too ill to attend services in the main church, and placed at a short but discreet distance from the abbey's cemetery. The sheer size of the infirmary is an indication of how many elderly laymen, many of whom would have been former benefactors of the abbey, chose to end their days here, in addition to the monks. This preponderance of the elderly and the dying at the abbey may have helped to induce an almost morbid obsession with death. It was by Abbot Hugh's special decree that prayers for the dead began to fill a large span of time in the abbey church. The list of deceased monks throughout the Cluniac empire for whom those prayers were regularly—and collectively—said came to number several thousand by the end of Hugh's abbacy. The order had come to embrace an extended family of the dead.

For the most part the abbey was a self-contained world. According to Christopher Brooke in *The Age of the Cloister* there was even a certain simplicity about the economic life of Cluny (at least in the abbey's heyday):

> Cluny's basic needs were corn, especially wheat, beans, milk, butter, cheese and honey; wax for candles; cloth for habits; sheepskins and pigskins for parchment; timber and stone for buildings and furniture. In vine-growing country, such as the heart of the Mâconnais . . . there were vineyards and grapes. From the large estates near the abbey came corn and wine in the enormous quantities needed to support a large community; from farther afield the produce came transformed already into money, with which the other needs could be purchased. Beans and vegetables such as were used in the eleventh century—onions and leeks, for instance, but not later discoveries such as cabbages or potatoes—were grown in the monastic garden and the home farms; milk in modest quantities was presumably to be had from the cows and goats of the neighborhood, and also butter and cheese. . . . [The] absence of sheep, or large flocks of any kind . . . seems to be partly due to the absence of meat from the diet, and the practice, in Benedictine and Cluniac communities in the eleventh and twelfth centuries, of buying cloth ready-made; and this meant too that for the most part the animals whose skin provided the parchment had to be purchased, no doubt at considerable cost. Candles for the monastic church were probably made from pure beeswax in the Middle Ages, and honey was extensively used to sweeten

the diet before the import of sugar began in the fifteenth century. Thus bees and beehives were an important part of a monastic economy. In every large community the fishponds were vital, providing some relief from the salt fish that seems to have played a heavy role in the monastic diet.

The community at Cluny in the mid-eleventh century was around one hundred men; by the time Abbot Hugh died in 1109 the number had risen to about three hundred.

Who were these relatively few monks who exerted such a disproportionate influence on the wider world? What kind of men were they who—in order to serve their God—were prepared to give up family, titles, money, possessions, personal freedom, the hope of children, and indeed most of the ordinary daily pleasures of life, and instead to submit to a highly rigid regime?

We know from charters and other records of the time that a great many monks had previously been feudal lords, great or small, or at least members of the ruling classes; some were even of royal blood. During the abbacy of Odilo one of the monks was a certain Cosimir of Poland, who remained at Cluny for seven years until being recalled to his native land in order to occupy the throne. During Hugh's abbacy the count of Mâcon, Guy II, who was a young married man, decided to enter the abbey bringing with him thirty of his loyal knights, while his wife and daughter were dispatched to the nearby convent of Marcigny along with the wives and daughters of the count's knights. It is not recorded what prompted this bizarre change of life, nor what the respective wives and daughters thought about the arrangement. Vassals of a local lord would have had little say in such a matter.

The era of the first two Crusades produced many other examples of noblemen abandoning the wider world in favor of

Cluny. A certain Bernard of Uxelles enjoyed a renowned career as a soldier before exchanging his sword for a cross and then rising within the abbey to become Cluny's grand prior, a position second in importance only to the abbot himself. An even more exotic military recruit to the abbey was the viscount of Bourges, Eudes Harpin, who joined a Crusade to the Holy Land, only to be captured and imprisoned in Baghdad. Eventually Eudes's family managed to ransom him, whereupon he made his way to Constantinople and then to Rome before deciding to end his days as a monk at Cluny. What appears to be true, judging from examples like these, is the extent to which religious faith, and its accompanying obsession with divine punishment, was capable of imposing a fearful tyranny on the medieval mind. Thus a monastery often satisfied a yearning for security which these unsettled times could provide in no other way. Cluny offered men such as Bernard of Uxelles and Eudes Harpin not only a safe haven here on earth but a glimpse of the stairway to paradise.

However, colorful characters like these can hardly have been typical of Cluny's brethren, and we need to assume that a high proportion of those who chose to enter the abbey were men who had led more modest and ordinary—but still privileged—lives. The feudal system would have tied serfs to their masters' lands, and they would have been far too valuable as laborers to be allowed to follow a religious calling. Besides, recruits to the abbey would have been expected to bring gifts with them, either of goods or property, which inevitably ruled out the vast majority of the peasant population. Monasteries were by and large for the ruling classes, at least prior to the twelfth century.

In traditional Benedictine monasteries like Cluny, many members joined as children, and all, except the apostate and the few who moved on to become bishops or hermits, left only by way of the cemetery. A large number of the monks, at least initially, were not there of their own free will.

A regular form of recruitment was through the institution of "oblates," children committed to the abbey by their parents. By arrangement with the abbey the parents would bring a young son here. The abbey chamberlain (who was responsible for the clothing, washing, and shaving of the monks) would greet them, after which he would remove the boy's normal clothing and replace it with a linen shirt and an oblate's habit. The parents and their child were then led into the presence of the abbot, where the formal document of oblation was read aloud to them and then signed by the parents (in itself an indication that they were unlikely to be from the illiterate masses). Finally the boy was required to hold a paten with a wafer, and a chalice with wine mixed with water, whereupon the abbot blessed a cowl and placed it over the boy's head. The new oblate was now considered to be a member of the monastic community.

There seems to have been no specified age at which a boy could be received as an oblate, but it would certainly have been during pre-adolescence since at the age of fifteen, or thereabouts, he could become a full novice. His early education, such as it was—like adding his treble voice to the choir—was over. He could now be introduced by the abbot to the Rule of St. Benedict, take his place in the common dormitory and refectory, and begin his novitiate—a time of training and probation—by learning the convoluted ways of the abbey: when to kneel, when to bow, when not to bow, who to address and how, when to stand and when to remain seated, and above all when to intone the wonderful Gregorian chants so that the sound of the monk's massed voices would fill that glorious church.

Finally, after a year or more as a novice depending on his age and maturity, he was allowed to take his monastic vows. Chastity, obedience, poverty—this was now his life. He would never be permitted a relationship with a woman. He would bend on all occasions to the authority of the abbot. And any property or valuable goods that might formerly have been his would be his no longer. He was instructed that henceforth he could call nothing "mine" except his father and mother (whom he rarely saw). As a further lesson in humility he might find himself accompanying the abbot after Sunday Mass to wash the feet of poor travelers who arrived at the abbey's gates, and to help distribute alms among them.

His clothes were handed to him by the chamberlain. These consisted of a pair of drawers, several pairs of socks, a long black woolen robe together with a leather belt, a scapular—a sleeveless outer garment worn above the robe, and to which a cowl could be attached—and a "frocus," a kind of shoulder cape worn above the scapular. Extra sheepskin clothing might be offered to him in the winter months. He was also given two pairs of shoes, one of which was lined with fur, and sheepskin gloves. Each Christmas he was given a new cowl and frocus, new socks at Martinmass, new shoes on Maundy Thursday, and robes and drawers as they were required. In addition he received his own writing tablets, a wooden comb, needles and thread, and a knife in a sheath. Every Tuesday clothes to be washed were placed in a chest in the cloister, the launderers being discreetly admitted to collect them while the monks were celebrating Mass, duly returning them cleaned and pressed on Saturdays.

Eating habits were regulated just as precisely. The Rule of St. Benedict stipulated that meat should only be eaten if illness required it. But by the eleventh century certain relaxations had crept in; fowl was widely considered not to fall under Benedict's dictum. The Rule also limited the quantity of food to be consumed: two meals each day (and only one during Lent and parts of winter), the first to be served at midday, the second at sunset, with the occasional supplement of a light snack of bread and a little wine early in the day. Each meal consisted of three courses—dried beans to start with (presumably in the form of some salad), followed by cheese and eggs (or sometimes fish), and finally fresh vegetables from the abbey garden. On special days onions accompanied by little cakes might replace the dried beans. On Good Friday the diet was punitively frugal, consisting of dry bread and raw vegetables. A cup of wine was allowed to each monk daily, and this might be supplemented on feast days (and there were a great many of these) with that favorite medieval beverage, hippocras, a rich concoction of red wine and spices.

Every monk had his own cup, either of metal or of wood, and all of them would be kept outside the refectory on the edge of the cloister, each covered in the summer months with a sprig of box-wood to ward off the flies. Close by there would be a twig of vine dipped in some kind of glue that acted as an effective flytrap.

Meals themselves were held in the main refectory. The monks remained standing until the abbot entered and took his place. Then they seated themselves at long tables set down the entire length of the room. But on a raised dais at one end of the refectory were three "high" tables, one being reserved for the grand prior and any guests he might invite, the second for the claustral prior (who was in charge of all domestic affairs), while the table in the middle was kept for the abbot himself and his guests, maybe some visiting abbot or other high-ranking churchman, or a duke or prince, or on occasions even the pope himself. The monks would then eat in silence while a reading was conducted.

Contemporary accounts of these day-to-day domestic matters may sometimes give us cause to be skeptical, particularly over the monks' eating habits. Just as not all monks remained celibate or poor, so a considerable (and increasing) number turned a blind eye towards the Rule when it came to matters of food. Standards undoubtedly slipped after Abbot Hugh's time, just as they did in other areas of monastic life, and increasingly drew fierce criticism from monastic reformers like Bernard of Clairvaux. The popular image of the jolly medieval monk, round of belly and pink of complexion, was not entirely the creation of later fiction.

But even though Cluny's official documents do not always tell the whole story, any more than do official biographies of its abbots, they at least outline with stark clarity what was *supposed* to happen at Cluny, and what most of the time probably *did* happen. Cluniac customaries, for example, allow us to piece together a typical monk's day.

The balance of such a day was between liturgical prayer and singing, contemplative prayer and reading, and work (though much of the menial work was gradually phased out largely due to lack of time, and delegated instead to lay brothers and servants). A monk's day was measured out by eight canonical hours—the Liturgy of the Hours—each announced by the bell and marked with a service in the abbey church or readings from the Bible. The timing of these hours would vary with the seasons; nonetheless, the order and observance of them were strictly kept, even—as much as was possible—by monks who were away on a journey. The hours tended to be counted from the moment of sunrise. Hence Matins was always sung at dawn, summer or winter; Prime was one hour later; Terce (the "third hour") two hours after that, followed at intervals through the day by Sext (the "sixth hour", around noon), None (the "ninth hour"), Vespers (at sunset), Compline (at nightfall), and Nocturns during the course of the night. There was very little uninterrupted sleep, and monks would sometimes have to be kept awake by means of a bright lantern held before them during night services.

When the bell rang for Nocturns the monks would rouse themselves from their beds (of straw, renewed once a year), taking great pains not to display any nakedness, after the service returning to bed with the same strict attention to modesty, only to be woken once again a few hours later. The bell for Matins at dawn prompted the same self-conscious routine, except that now after dressing themselves the monks made their way first to the cloister where they washed their hands and faces at the fountain, drying them on the towels provided, and finally running a comb through their hair before entering the church.

A typical winter day at Cluny began around 2 in the morning with psalms, and continued at least until 6 in the evening. At about 3.30 a.m. there would be a reading and two more psalms (apparently sung prostrate). A procession followed that was accompanied by chanting. Then more psalms around 5 a.m., and two more about 6 a.m. (again prostrate), after which the monks were permitted a very brief return to bed before it was time for Prime and four more psalms.

And so it went on throughout the day—a relentless timetable of ritual and routine. Around 7 in the morning there was a reading, psalms (prostrate) and a talk. At Terce more psalms. Then followed a period of (manual) work. Sext was at midday, with psalms and further work until None in the early afternoon. Lunch, the main meal of the day, might be as late as 2.30 p.m. Then another reading until Vespers with more psalms some time after 4 p.m., followed by a procession to the abbey church. Finally a light supper before Compline around 5 p.m.

These timings have been suggested by Joan Evans, though we have to bear in mind that this was an era before clocks. The keeping of hours must always have been approximate. The monks did have hourglasses, and probably tallow candles made to burn down after a prescribed period of time; but otherwise there was only the sundial, and that was of little use in bad weather, and of no use at night.

One feature of monastic life that was more or less invariable was the rule of silence. Speaking was strictly rationed throughout the day. And as a result of this rule of silence an elaborate hand-language of signs developed within the walls of the abbey, which had to be learnt by each new monk if he wanted to be able to communicate with his fellow brethren.

Conversation with the abbot, at least on important matters, was permitted at all times. In the chapter house after morning mass he would regularly preside. And after the statutory reading—a chapter from the Rule, and the occasional spiritual lecture—this would become the occasion for business matters concerning the abbey to be discussed, and discussed openly. It was also the occasion for any monk who had transgressed in some way to be invited to confess and to be duly punished.

Joan Evans has described a typical event of this kind in *Monastic Life at Cluny* when a monk would be summoned to the chapter house to answer for his misdoings:

> If he was convicted of a venial sin the Abbot ordered him to be beaten with a rod. After his chastisement he had to remain prostrate before the altar during the services, shut out from participating in the rites, excluded from the common table, until one of the brothers came from the Abbot to whisper in his ear, "You are absolved." If his sin was more serious—drunkenness, anger, swearing, quarrelling, calumny, pride, envy, covetousness, the possession of private property, perjury, absence from the monastery precincts without leave, malingering, speech with a woman, or other grave dereliction from

the Cluniac rule—the culprit had to stand at the Chapter-house door barefoot, his scapular and cape off and folded under his left arm, his robe undone, a bundle of rods in his right hand. When allowed to approach, he laid his garment and the rods on the floor, and prostrated himself to ask pardon. Then he was chastised until the Abbot said, "It is enough."

The severity with which brethren were treated for what may seem relatively minor offences is in vivid contrast to the generosity extended to outsiders. Guests who had arrived on horseback (usually the more prosperous ones) would be received at the abbey for three days without being expected to make any donation. Thereafter no doubt a contribution would be negotiated. The abbey's guesthouse provided lodging for up to forty men and thirty women, and a guest master was on hand to look after them. During their stay they could enjoy their own refectory with the services of a cook, stabling for their horses and a groom to take care of them, a porter, as well as other servants available to perform day-to-day menial tasks.

Those who arrived on foot were treated less grandly; nevertheless, they would be lodged—free of charge—outside the abbey in the town itself, and provided with bread and wine during their stay, and sometimes even with meat.

Pilgrims were especially welcomed, being invited to attend certain church services and to admire the holy relics that would be placed on display on special occasions. They were offered bread and wine, and as a matter of course received alms at the abbey's almonry; this fund was maintained regularly by one-tenth of all moneys collected in church (presumably from visitors) in addition to one-tenth of all income that was received in tithes from abbey property in the region. Given Cluny's fame and the number of pilgrims who would have made their way here, the abbey must have been an abundant charity.

A short distance from the great cloister was the abbey library, which in the early days was little more than a book cupboard (*armarium*). All books were handwritten on parchment and thus a rare treasure; they were highly valued at Cluny as part of a monk's religious education, and during the summer months two hours a day were set aside for the brethren to read in the cloister. With shorter days in winter this period was reduced to one hour, though on Sundays throughout the year monks could read whenever they wished, provided they could manage to find sufficient time in the abbey's packed liturgical schedule.

Because of the scarcity of books, much of the reading was public; passages from the Old Testament, the Acts of the Apostles, the book of Revelation, or the epistles of St. Paul, as well as St. Augustine, Cassian, and Gregory the Great, would be read aloud to the assembled monks. But also available, and mostly for private reading, was a more unexpected range of literature. In addition to the many lives of the saints and the writings of Jerome, Bede, Alcuin and other fathers of the church, the library possessed volumes on civil and canon law, history, arithmetic, music, and science, as well as the writings of "profane" classical authors such as Pliny, Livy, Vitruvius, and in particular Virgil. (Later, during the twelfth century, translations from the Arabic of books on astronomy and algebra were added.)

A place of special pride at Cluny was the scriptorium. The copying and illumination of manuscripts was one of the abbey's finest achievements, and was the only artistic activity actually practiced within the cloistered walls by the monks themselves. Manuscripts, once completed, would be bound together in the form of a book. Work took place in an area known as the "lesser cloister" under the supervision of the claustral prior. It was his responsibility to prepare the parchment for the scribes, having first obtained all necessary materials from the chamberlain. The scribes would then set to work. This was their only task; they would have learnt their skills as novices and proceeded to practice them for much of their lives, or at least so long as their eyesight held. The few Cluniac manuscripts that survive, in the British Museum in London and the Bibliothèque Nationale in Paris, bear witness to the extraordinary beauty of the writing that the monks achieved, particularly in the elaborately decorated initials with which each section of a manuscript begins.

One indication of the high esteem in which these scribes were held is the fact that they were the only group of monks who were at times excused from attending regular services—surprisingly in an institution where ritual and ceremony were so essential!

The rule of ritual at Cluny grew increasingly intense as the eleventh century progressed, until the chanting of psalms and the liturgical prayers, together with hymns, canticles, and readings from the Bible took up the greater part of the Cluniac day. The papal legate Peter Damian wrote to Abbot Hugh after one of his official visits to the abbey: "The offices succeeded each other with such rapidity that even in the long days of summer there remains only half an hour in which the brethren can talk in the cloister." There would seem to be an implied criticism here. However glorious the celebration of the Divine Office—and there can be no doubt that it was, the singing swelling up into that huge barrel-vaulted nave of the abbey church and drifting across the town and adjacent fields at all hours of the day and night—it was beginning to leave little time for anything else. There was scant opportunity for private study, prayer, or meditation. Liturgical duties were taking precedence over all other exercises of the spirit or mind.

More significantly, because it directly contravened the Rule of St. Benedict, there was no longer time for manual labor. Traditionally, several hours of a monk's day had been spent working, often in the abbey garden, tending the herbs and vegetables, weeding the neat geometrical plots that one can see in early drawings of Cluny, with the great abbey church in the background.

The contribution of the monastic orders to horticulture is huge, and that of the Benedictines greatest of all. Because of the prohibition to eat meat except on special occasions, monks became expert gardeners, providing fruit and vegetables for their kitchen as well as herbs for their infirmary. They were pioneers in the understanding of techniques such as soil enrichment, land reclamation and drainage, the cultivation of vineyards and orchards, and above all in the dissemination of knowledge of medical plants.

But at Cluny all such skills began to count for little. By the end of Abbot Hugh's abbacy most of the physical work in the garden and orchards had become delegated to lay brothers or to servants who belonged outside the monastery altogether. It was an issue that was soon to hand Cluny's enemies one of their sharpest weapons, and to Hugh's successors an uneasy legacy.

XII.

Vanitas Vanitatis

The death of Abbot Hugh in 1109 heralded the beginning of a long afterglow in the fortunes of Cluny, an afterglow which shone radiantly for a while, postponing the even longer night to follow.

No one chosen to succeed Hugh was ever going to find it easy. In his sixty years as abbot Hugh had never appointed regular subordinates; there was no line of succession, no deputy ready to step in to fill the vacuum.

Yet at first it must have seemed that the monks had decided well. The chosen successor was a young Languedocien by the name of Pons (or Pontius, in Latin). He was yet another well-connected aristocrat, the son of the count of Mergueil and a relative of Pope Paschal II. He enjoyed the extra prestige of having been called to the monastic life by Hugh himself. The choice of Pons promised continued stability; indeed it was recorded that "so eminent was his virtue that he was elected without a single dissentient voice."

During his early years as abbot the affairs of the Cluniac empire seemed to prosper much as before. There were now almost 1,500 dependant monasteries with 10,000 monks, scattered all over France, Germany, Spain, Italy, and Britain. The abbey's special privileges were confirmed by the pope yet again, and gifts of churches and priories were still coming Cluny's way, even if there were now fewer of them. Best of all, work on Hugh's great abbey church was continuing apace; it had become very much Abbot Pons's priority. The vast central portal, more than sixty feet high and with a magnificent array of carved figures, was finally brought to completion. At the same time a large new cloister was being created to the south of the church. Altogether Pons was showing himself to be a lavish patron of sculptors and masons, and a man who clearly loved beautiful things.

He also appeared to be a devout and pious man. Four years after his election Pons made the pilgrimage to Santiago de Compostela. Admittedly he scarcely did it in the spirit of a poor pilgrim, on foot and staff in hand, but with a retinue fit for a king. Nonetheless, he did it. Pons was not by any means alone in making the journey in such a triumphant fashion; the *camino*, the road through northern Spain to Santiago, was by now relatively safe, the Moors pushed back south and the bandits by and large removed. As a result, in addition to either being a journey of sincere faith, or to do penitence, as a punishment, in the hope of a miraculous healing, because of wanderlust, or for a number of other reasons, the *camino* was now attracting a new breed of pilgrim—the person of high rank enjoying a fashionable exercise in piety by going on a comfortable adventure in foreign parts, and perhaps whitewashing a few sins along the way.

Pons's piety took other forms as well. He persuaded the Italian cleric Gilo, believed to have been the bishop of Tusculum (near Rome) at the time, to write a biography of Abbot Hugh, and Gilo's work survives as the least hagiographical of the various accounts of the great man's life. It was also about this time that Cluny received from returning Crusaders three holy relics of unmatchable spiritual prestige: a fragment of the Holy Cross studded with precious stones, a finger of the first Christian martyr, St. Stephen, and a tooth of St. John the Baptist which Pons ordered to be suspended within a jeweled reliquary and displayed to the left of the high altar.

By now the new abbot's taste for excess must have been apparent to everyone within the somber walls of the abbey. But so far at least it all appeared to be richly in the service of God. At the same time, however, Pons had inherited a number of major challenges that became increasingly apparent. For the last twenty years of his abbacy Hugh had traveled less and less, eventually confining himself almost completely to the area around Cluny. Inevitably this meant a relaxation of control and supervision of daughter houses, where decisions were increasingly made behind the abbot's back. New monks were confessed without his leave and often without his knowledge, some of them soon proving to be quite unsuited to the rigors of monastic life. As a result standards of discipline throughout the order were dropping, while at the same time small local interests and local rivalries inevitably began to flourish.

On top of this, Pons did not possess his predecessor's gift for concealing an iron fist within a velvet glove. He was too arrogant a man to be a good diplomat; he was by nature a bully, and in consequence the number of his enemies began to grow. Relationships between the abbey and the local bishops (and archbishops) had always been tense because of the privileges Cluny enjoyed, and it had required all of Hugh's skills as a negotiator to keep those relationships within the bounds of civility.

To make things worse, the financial donations to the abbey were continuing to fall off. The exception, at least for the time being, was Spain. But since King Alfonso VI had died the same year as Hugh there was increasing doubt that the flow of Spanish gold would continue indefinitely. Payments were now often in arrears at just the time when the vast abbey church was nearing completion and expenses were exceptionally high.

In short, within a decade of his election it was becoming clear that Pons was faced with more than one potential crisis. He had few friends, dwindling support from church authorities, and dwindling funds—which for a man with his appetite for luxuries must have been the most uncomfortable blow of all.

At least relationships between Cluny and the papacy were at this stage still cordial enough. The continued existence of an antipope in Rome made the position of the "official" pope especially precarious, and he was more than ever reliant on the support (and hospitality) of Cluny. We know for instance that Pope Calixtus II, the former bishop of Vienne, in 1119 found himself actually elected to the papacy at Cluny. The new pope proceeded to spend a good deal of time at the abbey, and it was during his stay there, in 1120, that he canonized Hugh.

While at Cluny Calixtus invested Pons with his personal ring, then reaffirmed the right once given to Hugh of permitting the abbot to wear full pontifical regalia during Mass—purple gloves, a jeweled miter, and gold-embroidered shoes—and also agreed to Pons's presumptuous request that he be allowed to call himself "abbot of abbots," or "archabbot," an honor traditionally awarded only to the abbot of the very first Benedictine monastery at Monte Cassino.

There is a scarcity of records relating to the last period of Pons's thirteen-year abbacy. But colorful fragments of information do suggest that Pons was by now becoming thoroughly filled with self-importance. One eyewitness account shows him making the rounds of dependent abbeys, at one of which, at Abbeville in northern France, he arrived "in great pomp with a train of one hundred mules," and proceeded to throw his weight about to such an extent that the local abbot took deep offence.

We know that eventually Pons was removed from office. In 1122 Pope Calixtus took the unprecedented step in response to complaints by a body of monks of actually deposing the abbot of

Cluny. The complaints centered around Pons's personal extravagance and the waste of the abbey's wealth.

The events that followed the deposition of Pons are rather bizarre. The new abbot was a monk hardly in the first flush of youth, but who possessed a name which promised longevity—Hugh. However, Hugh II survived barely three months. The man who then succeeded him was a young nobleman of twenty-eight from the Auvergne, a great-nephew of the first Abbot Hugh. His name was Peter of Montboissier, later to become known as Peter the Venerable.

Peter was faced with an enormous challenge. Thanks in part to the extravagances of Pons, Cluny's finances were by now considerably diminished. Morale in the abbey was also at a low ebb; there was much internal disaffection in monastic ranks, while from outside fierce criticism towards the abbey for its supposed moral laxity and its obsession with material splendors was mounting.

Peter did his best. He was a conscientious man, humane and cultured, a theologian of considerable accomplishment, and often referred to—rightly so—as the last great abbot of Cluny. During the early years of his abbacy he spent much time painstakingly putting the affairs of the Cluniac empire back in order, visiting dependent houses, listening to complaints, reassuring the disaffected, placing prudent checks on expenditure, reestablishing monastic discipline.

But if his task was far from easy he could never have anticipated the great dramas ahead. In 1125, three years after his election, Peter undertook a diplomatic tour of Cluniac houses in Aquitaine, to the west of Burgundy. While he was absent from the abbey the disgraced Pons suddenly reappeared, with violent intent. We have an anonymous chronicler's account of what took place:

Having gathered round him certain fugitives, to whom he gave rustic arms, he [i.e., Pons] advanced unexpectedly towards the gates of Cluny, burst through them, drove away the monks with their old prior, Bernard, and with a mixed crowd of armed men and even women stormed the cloisters. . . . He then seized the holy ornaments, golden crosses, golden tablets, gold candelabras, gold incense bearers, vases of great weight, holy chalices, not even sparing the gold and silver boxes and shrines enclosing the martyrs' bones. From these and other articles he melted down an immense weight of gold with which to hire soldiers in the neighborhood . . . and proceeded to devastate the land with fire and sword.

We do not know how accurate this chronicler was, but it would appear that Pons had simply gone mad. Nonetheless, he did manage to reestablish himself, temporarily at least, as abbot of Cluny.

Pons may not have been universally opposed in his rampage; some of the monks—but in all likelihood not too many—might have been delighted to see so generous and worldly a man return to the seat of office.

It would take several months before Peter was able to restore order in Cluny and reclaim his position as abbot. Meanwhile the pope summoned both men to Rome to hear a personal account of these turbulent events. By this time the vanity of Pons had become utterly overweening, allowing him to protest loudly that "no living mortal could ever excommunicate him." The boast got him nowhere. The pope listened to his plea, then proceeded to pass sentence on him. He gravely described Pons as "usurper, sacrilegious, schismatic, excommunicate," then deprived him of all offices forever, and committed him to prison, where very shortly

Pons contracted a disease (probably malaria) and died. It was a sad and dishonorable end, just one year after his reckless assault on the abbey.

After Peter the Venerable had been duly restored as abbot of Cluny in 1126 he got on with the tasks and challenges that were now doubly taxing. On top of the financial burden he had inherited, Peter needed to set about repairing as best he could the moral and physical damage inflicted on the abbey by his crazed predecessor.

It is tempting to blame Pons for the many ills that crowded in on Cluny during those early decades of the twelfth century. And inevitably his outrageous behavior makes him the one villain in an otherwise upright and dignified procession of abbots who ruled there for the first two hundred and fifty years of Cluny's existence. At the same time we should not overlook that he was the man who had successfully brought the vast central portal of Cluny III to completion. It is possible to see Pons as also having a hand (though we have no supporting evidence) in the creation of another great portal of the period—one that miraculously has survived—at the Cluniac abbey church of Moissac, north of Toulouse.

Moissac was important in the Cluniac hierarchy, its abbot being second in seniority only to the abbot of Cluny himself. Since its annexation by Abbot Odilo early in the previous century Moissac had by now acquired more than seventy daughter houses of its own, and not surprisingly a good deal of wealth in the process.

Subsequent history has not treated Moissac all that well. The abbey was twice occupied, and presumably ransacked, by the English during the Hundred Years' War. It suffered further degradations during the Wars of Religion, and was then suppressed altogether during the French Revolution, its art treasures pillaged or disfigured during the Reign of Terror. In the mid-nineteenth century Moissac's Spanish-inspired cloister was saved by a whisker from being demolished to make room for the new Bordeaux-Sète railway.

The tympanum above the south portal at Moissac makes one regret even more the loss of the tympanum at Cluny. Certainly the Moissac sculptor—and we do not know who he was—looked to Burgundy for inspiration. Christ in Majesty is seated gravely in the center, above the lintel. Around him are the symbols of the four evangelists, while below him and on either side the familiar twenty-four elders of the Apocalypse are for once engaged in the action—they have set aside their musical instruments and turned their heads upwards in astonishment. Throughout the entire tympanum the sculptor has created an atmosphere of awestruck silence. This is sculpture as drama.

And yet, if the sculptor looked to Burgundy he did so with only one eye. With the other eye he gazed southwards over the Pyrenees to the art and architecture of Moorish Spain, with its hybrid mixture of Muslim and Christian influences. The twin doors of the portal are flanked by a pair of jagged columns, like a giant trap, or an open jaw set sideways, while in the center between the two doors rises a single vertical column known as a trumeau or pier. On this trumeau three pairs of rampant lions are most delicately carved, one pair above the other, each pair intertwined to create an "X." The impact of the whole portal is almost frightening; it makes one want to recoil rather than pass between those open jaws. Maybe more than one sculptor worked on the Moissac portal, each bringing with him a different tradition and different skills. Certainly this extraordinary trumeau of the six intertwined lions has nothing whatever in common with the art of Burgundy—if anything it echoes the early sculptures on ancient Assyrian temples. In all probability a more direct source of inspiration would have been the illustrations to Beatus's eighth-century *Commentary on the Apocalypse*, which were specially popular among Spanish painters and sculptors at this time.

But the most striking feature of the Moissac portal is all but hidden as one stands facing those twin doors. On the lion column's two sides, flattened into the stone so that they only become visible as one passes under the lintel, are two full-size figures, on the left the apostle Paul and on the right the prophet Jeremiah. Paul is stern—appropriately—while Jeremiah is gentle and reflective. Both are carved in deep gray granite, and with a lightness of touch that suggests they could be dressed in silk. They are elongated, giving a delicate sensation of movement to each figure. Hair and beard carry the same sense of movement, each strand of hair finely etched in the stone as if actually combed. Jeremiah's body is twisted, his head turned slightly so that he looks away from us lost in thought, an expression of benign sadness on his face. He is the prophet who sees only doom, and can do nothing about it.

This is sculpture that searches deep, laying bare something of the human soul. Only the greatest artists in any era have made intractable stone express the inner self—and the sculptor of these Moissac figures is one of them. Few examples of European art portray so eloquently the passionate and mystical nature of the medieval religious experience. This is Cluniac art at its finest, matched only by two other sculptural masterpieces—the great portals of the abbey church at Vézelay and the cathedral of St. Lazare at Autun, both in Burgundy, and both intimately connected to Cluny.

XIII.

Peter the Venerable

 To have been known as "the Venerable" even in his own lifetime must have placed a solemn burden of expectation on Abbot Peter. Yet the very label "Venerable" is a measure of the respect felt for this most scholarly of medieval churchmen.

Peter's abbacy is the hardest of all to evaluate, largely because the very real achievements of his thirty-four years in office have tended to be overshadowed by dramatic outside events and challenges that drew him in inexorably, though often unwillingly. Chief among these were, firstly, the bitter schism in Rome between Pope Innocent II and the antipope Anacletus II; then the rumbling and very public dispute between the Cluniacs and the Cistercians sponsored by that unforgiving ascetic Bernard of Clairvaux; and finally the even-more-public issue of the hapless philosopher Peter Abelard, whom Bernard hounded and Peter chose to shelter.

Peter's two most distinguished predecessors, Odilo and Hugh, had enjoyed a combined period of office lasting an astonishing one hundred and fifteen years. Perhaps their remarkable longevity was assisted by the fact that both men had inherited a flourishing and expanding monastic empire. Peter the Venerable was far less fortunate—the empire was now coming under increasing attack. Its values as well as its practices were being questioned from many sides, both within and outside the church, and its power and influence were on the wane. The somewhat crude feudal society into which Cluny had been born, and whose very crudeness had helped it flourish, was already much changed, becoming more complex and in many ways more sophisticated. Centers of power were shifting, both politically and intellectually. The rise of large cities, with their growing commercial wealth and fledgling universities, meant that the Benedictine world of little rural fortresses of faith was beginning to seem old-fashioned and out of touch. Christendom no longer felt itself to be under siege—at least not on home territory.

Besides, the monastic mood itself was changing. In reaction to the gloss and the elaborate ceremonies cultivated to an almost obsessive degree by the Cluniacs, there was now a yearning to return to the kind of basic values and pure faith that had been preached by the early fathers of the church. Hence the growing appeal and influence of the new reform movement of the Cistercians, for whom a personal and reflective relationship with God was far more important than elaborate church services involving displays of bejeweled images and the interminable chanting of psalms.

When Peter returned to office in 1126 he was not only faced with these challenges of the larger world—he had also inherited something approaching an economic crisis in the affairs of Cluny. His first responsibility after clearing up the moral and physical destruction left by his deranged predecessor was to try to balance the abbey's books. Over the previous hundred years the Cluniac order had expanded so dramatically, both in the number of religious houses it embraced and the plethora of lands and other properties it owned, that it was now in severe danger of becoming top-heavy. In material terms the order was simply too big; the expense as well as the burden of administering such a far-flung empire were weighing heavily on the mother abbey, especially now that donations were becoming fewer, and in consequence the abbey's revenues—its liquid assets—were diminishing year by year.

It remains immensely to Peter's credit that through insistence on efficient management he was able to stabilize the abbey's finances for virtually the entire period he was in office. By openly supporting Pope Innocent II against the antipope in Rome Peter ensured that Cluny was richly rewarded by having its vital privileges confirmed, and even extended. One such privilege the abbey managed to acquire was that all monks and townspeople alike, including pilgrims, visiting merchants, and other travelers to Cluny, should be exempt from the requirement to pay the customary tolls—making it a kind of duty-free area. The result was an economic boost both to the abbey itself and to the community at large.

On the face of it, then, the abbey under Peter appeared to be still going from strength to strength. At least it was certainly doing so in terms of numbers—the community of monks continued to grow. When Innocent II, during his protracted stay at Cluny, dedicated the all-but-completed abbey church (Cluny III) in 1130 he did so in an atmosphere of self-confidence and well-being. Two years later an English chronicler and historian, Orderic Vitalis, could write of a procession of 1,212 monks "singing and with heartfelt joy raising their eyes to God—and I write this with certainty," he added, "because I had the happiness to be among them."

The occasion must have been some very special event in which delegations from numerous daughter houses would have attended a service at the newly dedicated abbey church; not even Cluny could boast a community of over a thousand. Nonetheless, we know that by the end of Peter's abbacy, in the 1150s, the community numbered more than 450 resident monks.

What is certain is that building work in Peter's time, and already during Pons's rule, had by no means been confined to the new abbey church. Cluny was an altogether more comfortable place than before. Novices had their own separate living quarters arranged around their own cloister. The growing number of lay brothers likewise enjoyed their own separate quarters, and these were conveniently situated close to the stables and various workshops where they were employed. Since the monks themselves no longer performed most manual tasks there was now a need for an extensive labor force of lay brothers skilled in just about everything from shoeing horses to making wine.

While life at Cluny for the monks had long achieved a certain ease and comfort, a poignant corrective can be found in the person of a monk by the name of Bernard of Morlaix. He was a poet and moralist, possibly English or maybe Breton in origin, who came to Cluny during the time of Peter the Venerable in order to study literature and theology, as a result of which he proceeded to set down his verdict on the human race in poetic form. The result of these labors of a great many years were numerous Latin verses dedicated to the Virgin Mary, but most of all a poem in dactylic hexameter of some three thousand lines, dedicated to Abbot Peter himself and entitled *De Contemptu Mundi*, "On Condemning the World." The poem is exactly that—a passionate condemnation of just about every conceivable human pleasure in our material world, all of them described in lurid apocalyptic imagery that—so it has been claimed—may have exerted some influence on Dante's *The Divine Comedy*.

The presence of such a misanthrope within the walls of Cluny is a reminder that the humane values propounded by its great abbots, in particular Hugh and Peter, were not the only views that found a voice within the Cluniac empire. One even senses from the very existence of Bernard of Morlaix that the mood at Cluny may have been changing. Instead of being "the light of the world" of

Pope Urban II, the abbey—or at least one section of it—was in danger of retreating from that world, choosing darkness rather than light, the way back rather than the way forward. The monastic orders had always found difficulties reconciling spirituality with a thriving secular world. Now it was as if those gloomy voices within Cluny longed to take a leaf out of the Cistercian book and remove the monastery as far as possible from the bustling urban life with its distractions and temptations, but also its glories. It may be no accident that even as sophisticated and scholarly a man as Peter the Venerable as he grew older felt the need to retreat, not to delightful Berzé in the sunlit Mâconnais hills as Hugh loved to do, but to a colony of hermits deep in the woods of the Charolais. Here, Peter wrote, "wearied with living in towns we live in the forest and love the meadows."

However, it is reasonable to assume that no abbot of Cluny would have condemned himself to wearing goatskin and living in a cave, as medieval hermits traditionally did—or at least as they were popularly depicted as doing in early paintings. The hermitage to which Peter retreated is more likely to have been a modest farmhouse shorn of all but basic comforts, and—perhaps more importantly—shorn of the burden of daily ritual and the heavy responsibilities of high office. What seems significant is the spirit of weariness that induced Peter to seek a retreat into the comforts of nature. Whereas with Abbot Hugh the burdens of the world had always appeared a challenge to be welcomed, however heavy they might be, with Peter those burdens more often appeared to be a yoke, however light.

One burden about which Peter must have had very mixed feelings concerned the ancient monastery of Baume-les-Messieurs, Cluny's parent house. Towards the end of Peter's abbacy he received a letter from the pope, Eugenius III, informing him of an "execrable

and horrible crime" which had been committed by the monks of
Baume on "our beloved son Master Osbert." As a result he had
decided to entrust the aforesaid abbey along with all its lands and
treasures to the abbot of Cluny so that henceforth the place "be
ordered and run as a priory." Meanwhile several members of
Baume, both monks and priests, were to be excommunicated for
having disobeyed papal orders.

Little is known about Master Osbert except that he was not
apparently a monk; most probably he was a papal messenger, or
nuntius, traveling maybe on some matter relating to religious
reform, or perhaps to sort out a local ecclesiastical dispute. As to
the "execrable and horrible crime" committed against the
unfortunate Osbert, so appalling must it have been that a blanket
of silence was thrown over the matter, so preventing any danger of
a historical record revealing its exact nature. It was four years after
the pope's original statement before Abbot Peter could bring
himself to refer to it at all, and then only as "the case which is all
too well known to men of our time, and which owing to the
disgrace of it should not be transmitted in writing to posterity."

Clearly the matter continued to rumble on, because several
decades later a subsequent pope wrote of "the unheard of savagery
of the monks of Baume" in committing "their evil deed." Was it
merely some humiliating derobing as a deliberate insult to the
papacy, or indeed a sexual assault, even a castration, as some
historians have suggested? Perhaps Peter the Venerable passed the
most apt verdict on the matter when he observed about monastic
life in general that it would take an entire book to describe the
assaults made by demons on his monks.

As for the abused Master Osbert we know next to nothing
about his subsequent career except that he received a pension for
life. Abbot Peter, meanwhile, now found himself the recipient of five

dependent monasteries, together with all their lands and goods, all of which had formerly belonged to the disgraced monastery of Baume: and among those goods was a remunerative source of that most sought-after of medieval commodities, one that brought flavor to the most meager diet, acted as a crucial preservative, and disguised food that was rotten—namely, salt.

Early in 1142 Peter made a long-planned visit to Spain at the invitation of King Alfonso VII, grandson of the monarch who had been Cluny's most important benefactor, Alfonso VI. The official purpose of the journey was to make a tour of inspection of all the Cluniac houses in the Iberian peninsula, most of which had been acquired during the abbacy of Hugh half a century before. As the visit was likely to be a protracted one Peter took the precaution of appointing a caretaker for all Cluniac affairs in the person of the archbishop of Bordeaux—no doubt he had learnt his lesson from Pons's attempted takeover in 1125. A senior outside authority clearly offered better security than leaving the place in the hands of the grand prior, which would have been the normal practice.

Peter was away from Cluny for an entire year. He had a large retinue with him, and the tour of inspection took in Le Puy, Moissac, and Roncesvalles on the way to Spain, then Pamplona, Estella, Nájera, Carrión de los Condes, and almost certainly Sahagún. The route he followed was the traditional pilgrim road to Santiago de Compostela, and Peter had always intended to go as far as Santiago itself to visit the shrine of the apostle St. James. It might have been bad weather that prevented him from doing so, or the pressing need to meet King Alfonso on urgent financial matters— the pledged two thousand gold coins a year to Cluny were by now seriously in arrears. But there was a third reason, one that seems entirely consistent with what we know of Peter—because it was during his tour of Spain that he conceived his big plan. Peter was a theologian and a scholar. Accordingly his plan revolved around written texts. And the texts that concerned him most were Islamic.

Unlike a great many contemporary churchmen and theologians Peter was no narrow-minded dogmatist for whom the Bible and the writings of the saints were the only source of truth and human knowledge. He was well aware that in the fields of mathematics, the physical sciences, and philosophy Islamic scholars were pre-eminent, and that within the more enlightened areas of the Christian world there was a new and growing desire to learn from them, however resistant the more conventional church leaders might be to such an idea. Translations from the Arabic were beginning to become available, the center of these new Islamic studies being the Spanish capital city of Toledo, which had been captured from the Moors some fifty years earlier. The city possessed rich libraries of Islamic books, and these libraries became the source of study by scholars and translators who were gathered round an enlightened archbishop, Raimondo. In fact Toledo had become a hive of intellectual inquiry among laymen and churchmen alike, all of them hungry to gain access to so much newly available knowledge. And after four hundred years of Muslim rule Arabic remained its common language.

It was Peter's awareness of this vibrant state of affairs that sparked the idea that was to remain in the forefront of his mind for the remainder of his life. It was a complex idea, appropriate for a complex man whose mind was an unusual combination of intellectual rigor and an unworldly naïveté. He was "indignant that Christians did not know Islam," he wrote. In his view Muslim learning and scholarship were welcome and admirable things, and

Christendom had much to benefit from appreciating them. What was regrettable was that such knowledge was supposedly under the banner of Islam, this religion being in Peter's conviction "a human error." If only he could open Muslim eyes to the teachings of Christianity, he thought, then all that scholarship and scientific knowledge would be seen to be in the service of the "one true religion," and all would be well with the world.

Islam needed to be resisted, Peter believed, not by force of arms but by force of argument, persuasion, and the power of reason. The very notion of a "holy war" repelled him. He proclaimed himself to be a man of peace. Muslims, he argued, should not be approached "as people often do, by arms, but by words; not by force, but by reason, not by hatred, but with love."

To Peter the Crusades were the wrong way; instead, the human intellect was the weapon he would choose. And his principal target would be the Qur'an. If a translator could be found to render it in Latin then he would be able to study the holy book of Islam and in doing so he could "refute" it—and thus the hideous war between Christians and Muslims could be won without further bloodshed. Consequently, he decided to commission the first translation of the Qur'an into Latin.

He began by identifying potential translators who were fluent in both Arabic and Latin. They turned out to be a colorful and varied lot. One was a Dalmatian with the unlikely name of Herman who was in Spain studying Arabic treatises on astronomy. Peter encountered him "around the River Ebro," and appears to have lured him towards working on the Qur'an by means of a handsome fee. The man was, he said, "a scholar of the most incisive literary genius." Then there was a certain Master Peter of Toledo, who seems likely to have been a morisco—a Christian Moor—as well as a Peter of Poitiers who was a Cluniac monk and therefore possibly the man who had introduced the abbot to the others. There was also a Muslim translator named Mohamed who was on hand to advise on the precise meaning of certain Arabic words.

But the key member of the group was an Englishman, Robert of Ketton. He was a priest and a noted scholar, and he had been translating Arabic scientific writings into Latin for some time, principally works on astronomy and mathematics. In fact his translation of a work on algebra is said to have been responsible for introducing the subject to the rest of Europe. It seems more than likely that Robert was already working on the Qur'an, or at least that he was closely familiar with it, since we know that the translation which bears his name as its principal author was finished only a few months after Peter's return to Cluny in 1143.

Now that Peter had the great book before him, his "refutation" could begin. In retrospect it is easy to see that Peter was pursuing an unobtainable objective from the very beginning. It says something about the static, fundamentalist state of the medieval mind that it seems never to have occurred to him that his mission was simply impossible. Quite apart from the naïveté of assuming that Muslims could be brought into the Christian fold simply by reasoned argument, Peter failed to understand that the Qur'an is believed by the faithful to be literally the word of God—it is his final revelation of the divine truth as dictated to Muhammad through the instruction of the angel Gabriel, and delivered in Arabic as God's chosen language. There could be no answers to this, and no room for argument. Strictly speaking the Qur'an could not even be translated. Scientific studies could quite legitimately be rendered from Arabic into Latin, but certainly not the holy words of God.

Peter's *Summa Totius Haeresis Saracenorum* ("Summary of all the Heresies of the Saracens") begins somewhat coyly: "A certain Peter, by nationality a Frenchman, by faith a Christian, by profession an abbot of those who are called monks, to the Arabs, the sons of Islam, who observe the law of one who is called Muhammad." "It seems strange," he goes on, "and perhaps it really is, that I, a man so very distant from you in place, speaking a different language, having a state of life separate from yours, a stranger to your customs and way of life, should write from the far parts of the West to men who inhabit the lands of the East and South, and that I should attack, by my utterance, those whom I have never seen, whom I shall perhaps never see." The effort to strike a note of tolerance and good will is very clear—at least until he gets to the nub of the matter, where his words turn deeply ignorant and offensive.

It is hard to say whether or not Peter's *Summa* made any real impact, and if so on whom. Certainly it would have bolstered the dogmatic antagonism of most Christian leaders toward Islam; but it is doubtful whether many of them even bothered with Peter's writings. Not surprisingly the *Summa* failed even to be translated into Arabic. Peter's great mission never got off the ground.

XIV

Battling Bernard of Clairvaux

The Cluny that Peter the Venerable had inherited in the 1120s was unique in a number of respects. It was unequalled in the breadth and scope of its monastic empire, stretching as it did across much of Europe and as far as the Holy Land. And in proportion to the quantity of properties it administered—and in many cases built—Cluny had also become a patron of the arts on a massive scale, not only in the fields of architecture and sculpture, but in mural painting, music, manuscript illumination, and all aspects of the decorative arts, from fine metalwork and ivory carving to the most elaborate gilding and enameling. In addition the abbey possessed one of the richest libraries in Europe, including works of classical literature and Latin translations of the Greek philosophers, soon to be supplemented at Peter's instigation by scientific works on astronomy and algebra translated from the Arabic.

Altogether the abbey had become not simply a monastery but a seat of learning, where respect for knowledge extended far beyond the conventional study of theology and the lives of the saints. Cluny had moved a considerable distance from being the sheltered island of simple prayer and plainsong it had once been. Now, with a scholar as its abbot it had begun to acquire much of the sophistication and intellectual vitality associated with the emerging universities.

At the same time just about everything Cluny had become by the early twelfth century was guaranteed to cause grave offence to the new Benedictine order, the Cistercians, and in particular to its leader, Bernard, Abbot of Clairvaux. Theirs was quite a different world. The classics, science, philosophy, art, rich decoration, sumptuous displays, elaborate rituals and ceremonies—the Cistercians turned their backs on all such intellectual and material temptations which they considered to be dangerous diversions of the mind.

The Cistercian order was named after the Burgundian abbey of Citeaux, which had been founded in 1097 or 1098 by Robert of Molesme as an ascetic alternative to Cluny. The choice of site, halfway between Beaune and Dijon, was significant—an inhospitable area of marsh and swamp (*cistels* means "reeds") which symbolized the determination of the founding monks to remove themselves as far as possible from the fleshpots of this world and to lead a spiritual life in which the Rule of St. Benedict could once again be followed in its most austere and simple form.

The new order might well have trodden a narrow and perhaps insignificant path had it not attracted a remarkable Englishman by the name of Stephen Harding. He became abbot of Citeaux in or about 1109, and in 1112 had the foresight to admit to his struggling and poverty-stricken community a group of some thirty young Burgundian noblemen, who had been persuaded to join the abbey by one of their number, a man by the name of Bernard (born around the year 1090). The band of followers who chose to join him in a life of the severest hardship included several of his brothers as well as an uncle and two cousins. It is hard to imagine today the emotional climate in which a large section of a privileged and well-off family would voluntarily give up everything—money, social position, marriage, a life of ease and privilege—in favor of an existence of acute physical deprivation for the sake of their burning faith. It is a state of affairs that demonstrates clearly the power a religious life was capable of exerting in those insecure times. What it also demonstrates is that Bernard's powers of persuasion were clearly quite extraordinary, even at this youthful age.

Three years later, in 1115, Abbot Harding appointed Bernard to lead a small group of monks to establish a sister monastery some eighty miles away just beyond the northern borders of Burgundy, at Clairvaux. With Bernard in charge of the new abbey the scene was now set for what was to become one of the great ideological struggles of the Middle Ages—a tussle between two giants of the medieval church, Bernard, the first abbot of Clairvaux, and Peter the Venerable, the ninth abbot of Cluny. The issue over which they clashed was a fundamental one: how should a servant of God best lead a Christian life?

By the time Peter was fully restored as abbot in 1126 Bernard had spent eleven years at Clairvaux, leading a life of the bleakest austerity, in a state of permanent ill health, which could hardly have been more different from the relatively sybaritic comfort and sophistication of Cluny. The battle lines were clearly drawn.

A remarkable feature of the feud between Peter and Bernard was that they managed—while publicly letting forth torrents of rhetorical accusation and self-justification over the decades to follow—nonetheless to remain friends all their lives, or at least to retain a deep mutual respect for one another. The correspondence between the two men spans more than a quarter of a century, ending only one year before Bernard's death in 1153 (Peter himself dying just three years later). Their letters cover a broad spectrum of leading issues of the day, chief among them the schism in Rome between pope and antipope, the turmoil surrounding the disastrous Second Crusade (which Bernard was to promote in a famous sermon at Vézelay in 1146), the threat of Islam in general, and of course the differences between the monastic ideals and practices of the two rival orders.

Though private in intent, theirs is a correspondence that in a sense was conducted in public, both authors taking care to have copies made for wider circulation. We can feel each man jockeying for position, rallying support, counting the points scored, always with an eye on power and position. The exchange of letters was invariably accompanied by a sense of history on both sides, echoing the celebrated correspondence between St. Augustine and St. Jerome. Peter tended to adopt Augustine's voice of wisdom and experience, calmly assuming the high moral ground by parading his scholarly understanding of the classical poets and philosophers whom he knew Bernard despised as pagan without ever having read them. On the other side there was Bernard's Jerome-like voice from the desert, alternately strident and gentle, authoritarian, fiercely self-righteous, but often engagingly perceptive and inclined always towards mysticism and a trust in the unique personal experience of religious faith which required—as far as he was concerned—none of Peter's scholarship to support it.

At times the tone of their letters hints at an important shift of power that had steadily been taking place between the two monastic orders. At the beginning of their relationship Bernard and his Cistercians were still struggling to survive, whereas Peter's Cluny, financially strained though it was, nevertheless still strode the monastic world like a colossus. But within two decades the balance had shifted dramatically. In that time Bernard had risen to become the most influential churchman of his day, the confidant of five popes, a mediator in numerous ecclesiastical disputes and court cases, and an advisor to kings and princes right across the continent—a role, ironically, which mirrored the one formerly held by Peter's great predecessor at Cluny, Abbot Hugh.

It was not that Cluny had hitherto been entirely alone in the campaign to tighten the discipline of the monasteries. Throughout the tenth and eleventh century reform had been in the air. In Germany the most powerful center of reform was the abbey of Hirsau, in the Black Forest, which came to impose Cluniac reforms on more than thirty monasteries, mostly in the south of the country, without actually becoming a dependency of the mother abbey. Besides Hirsau, another center of monastic reform was the great monastery of Gorze, near Metz, which was then also part of Germany. The importance of Gorze can be measured by the number of subservient religious houses that were reformed under its guidance—more than 160.

Nonetheless, until the rise of the Cistercians Cluny had remained the dominant force for reform in the monastic world. But now it was no longer. The expansion of the Cistercian movement was rapid and phenomenal (due, at least in part, to their spectacular success in farming the most inhospitable land, and for opening their doors to men of every social rank). Within three decades of its beginnings, up until the middle of the twelfth century, the number of Cistercian abbeys soared to 338; and 68 of these were founded directly by Clairvaux. This was their golden age, and suddenly there was a *new* white mantle of churches across Europe, a landscape of severe and elegant houses of God, many of them in the early Gothic style, and all of them devoid of ornament or decoration—in sharp contrast to the churches of Cluny.

The culmination of Cistercian power and influence came in 1145 with the election of a devoted disciple of Bernard's (and former novice at Clairvaux) as Pope Eugenius III. Whereas it used to be Cluny that could claim to have its own man in the Vatican, now that claim was Bernard's. Nor was he exactly shy in acknowledging the personal nature of the triumph: "People are saying," he wrote to

Eugenius, "that you are not the pope, but that I am." Bernard, so quick to condemn all manifestations of material luxury in others, was never one to deny himself the luxury of power. Humility and arrogance went hand in hand in the character of the man.

At the heart of the dispute between Cluny and Clairvaux lay the question of how strictly life should be led in accordance with the Rule of St. Benedict. Because Benedict had written not so much a rigid rule book but rather a series of essentially humane guidelines for his own monastic community at Monte Cassino, the Rule lent itself to a fairly broad range of interpretations. The Cisterians "took the Rule off the shelf," notes Christopher Brooke, "and read it as if it had just been written; they tried to forget the accretion of customs that had gathered round it elsewhere, and to follow Benedict to the letter . . . they were extremely austere; they pursued an ideal based on the personal pursuit of perfection." They chose to emphasize those aspects of the Rule that appealed to the ascetic temperament of their leader—seclusion and self-sufficiency. Their goal was to live as far as possible removed from centers of wealth and power, to exist on the most frugal of diets, to cultivate the land (the more inhospitable and challenging the better), and always to sleep in rough undyed vestments on wooden planks covered with straw in a common dormitory. The Cistercians were the monastic puritans of the twelfth century.

This severe and relentless equation of personal discomfort with spirituality was never one that the Cluniacs had chosen to embrace. If Bernard regarded such things as philosophy and classical literature as a distraction from the spiritual life, then Peter the Venerable would have regarded physical discomfort as a far more serious and quite unnecessary distraction.

Nevertheless, to some extent Bernard's cult of austerity echoed a prevailing mood of the time. The Cistercians were not alone in turning their backs on the pleasures of the material world. In 1084, fourteen years before the foundation of Citeaux, a teacher by the name of Bruno had voluntarily given up a teaching post in Reims and retreated with a group of disciples to the most isolated region of the Alps he could find, where he proceeded to set up a silent monastery among the snow-covered peaks which was to become La Grande Chartreuse, the motherhouse of the Carthusian Order. The legend of the early Christian hermits, with its accompanying myth of the desert, exerted a powerful grip on the religious imagination of the time, as though in some mystical way the untouched purity of nature could facilitate the purity of man's relationship with God. Bernard could even write as though he were a twelfth-century Rousseau, Wordsworth, or Thoreau: "Believe me, for I know, you will find something far greater in the woods than in books. Stones and trees will teach you things which you cannot learn from the masters."

Therein lies the gulf between the two men: Abbot Peter—the scholar, the intellectual, the classicist, the believer in reason, the man whose library was among the richest in Christian Europe—would have felt no sympathy at all with Bernard's rustic sentiments except as an occasional retreat from the real world. Peter's own periods of sojourn in the forest and meadows in the company of hermits were a necessary restorative, never a permanent way of life.

Not surprisingly during his early visits to Cluny Bernard took profound exception to much that he observed there. He was appalled by what he considered to be the abbey's overindulgence in food, and he was equally disgusted by the monks' fondness for lavishly decorated vestments. The architecture of the place offended him, too. The polished elegance of the columns in the church ambulatory (almost certainly the very ones that have survived) made him angry, while the floor of the choir, decorated with images of the saints in fine mosaic, roused his sardonic contempt. "Men spit sometimes in an angel's face," he wrote, "while often the countenance of some saint is ground under the heel of a passerby."

Bernard's furious outburst of disapproval, while directed at Cluny, pinpoints one of the fundamental divides within Christianity as a whole, namely the relationship of material beauty (art, ornament, decoration, visual richness) to the spiritual life: can material splendor, in whatever form, lead people to God, or does it merely act as a distraction? Are works of art in the service of God or in the service of mammon? The Cluniacs believed the former— the Cistercians the latter.

The issue is such a universal one, leaving its imprint on Western culture across the centuries, that there can be no easy answer. The purity of the Cistercian vision led to a glorious geometric simplicity of architecture typified by, for example, Rievaulx Abbey in Yorkshire and the abbey of Le Thoronet in Provence. One could speculate that if the Cluniac ethic had remained unchallenged such early-Gothic Cistercian masterpieces would never have existed; elaborate imagery and ornament would have radically altered the nature of them. On the other hand, had Cistercian purism prevailed everywhere and forever there would have been no sixteenth-century St. Peter's Church in Rome, no Michelangelo, no Bernini, and certainly no Titian or Rembrandt.

In the year 1124 Bernard delivered a celebrated sermon that was aimed specifically at Cluny. "I say nothing of the height of your churches, their immoderate length, their superfluous breadth, the costly polishings, the curious carvings and paintings which attract the worshipper's gaze and hinder his attention. . . . At the very sight of these expensive yet marvelous vanities men are more inclined to offer gifts than to pray." Again Bernard stresses the difference between the two orders—his emphasis rests on the central importance of prayer, which is essentially a private matter, whereas at Cluny the priority was always the liturgy, the elaborate church service with chanting and ceremony, which was by its very nature communal.

Bernard elaborated his stern sentiments relating to monastic life in a longer diatribe that he issued three years later. This was his *Apologia*, carefully not addressed to Peter the Venerable personally, though obviously for his attention above all, but framed as a letter to a fellow Cistercian, William of St. Thierry. Now he broadened his criticisms of Cluny to embrace every form of excess he found the abbey guilty of, including what the monks consumed in the refectory and what they wore in the abbey church. "They have satiety instead of food," he insisted, "and seek not clothing but adornment." With a special rebuke to Abbot Peter he declared that none of his predecessors would ever have permitted such excesses— and he pointedly named Odo, Mayeul, Odilo, and Hugh.

The style of Bernard's attack is often satirical, and invariably rhetorical, as though each sentence was designed to be declaimed from the pulpit—which it probably was, Bernard being especially fond of delivering sermons. "How do they keep the Rule," he challenged, "who are clad in furs, who, being healthy, feed on meat and the fat of meat, who allow three or four meals in one day, which the Rule forbids, who do not perform manual labor, which it orders, who in short change, or increase, or diminish many aspects of it according to their will?"

Everywhere Bernard looked he found what he considered to be complacency and lack of rigor about the way of life at Cluny. And his disgust is rarely hidden. "What is this freedom from care?" he thundered. "To recline over lengthy meals, or to wallow naked in a soft bed?" But then every so often the rhetorical bombast eases and his prose sharpens into a memorable phrase to describe what has caught his disapproving eye, as when he refers to "hands that are delicate with leisure."

Bernard's most telling criticism of Cluny was reserved for the issue of manual labor, though this was also the one Peter chose to defend most vigorously. Bernard was not alone in pointing out that the ever-increasing elaboration of Cluniac forms of worship, with its attention to pomp and show and its laborious rituals and interminable church services, left little or no time for anything else—private study, meditation, discussion, and in particular daily manual labor as prescribed as an important activity in the Rule of St. Benedict.

Bernard's charge that Cluny was deliberately breaking the Rule was, strictly speaking, unanswerable. In this respect the Cistercians obeyed the Rule to the very letter; they set great store by their efforts to tame and make productive the inhospitable environments in which they chose to live. Strenuous manual work was a positive virtue in their eyes; it was what St. Benedict had had in mind, and it was the way forward—hardworking, practical, down-to-earth, a life without superfluous luxuries. By contrast the Cluniac regime was seen as deviant, out of touch with reality, more inspired by the lifestyle of the secular aristocracy then the lives of the hermits and ascetics, irrelevant to the spiritual life, above all cluttered with pointless ritual that merely blinded a man to what really mattered.

In response Peter—the scholar, the man of letters—mounted a spirited defense. His argument was a subtle one, well chosen to emphasize the strengths of Cluny rather than its weaknesses, and the limitations of the Cistercian ideal. For Peter manual work was for laborers, not monks; digging the soil had little to do with God; there could be no special virtue in getting one's hands dirty. His own special pride lay in the abbey's scriptorium. Altogether his defense was elegant and to the point: "It is more noble," he wrote, "to set one's hand to the pen than to the plow, to trace divine letters on the page than furrows in the fields."

At this stage the contest would seem to be evenly matched, perhaps with Peter making the better of the arguments. His fullest response to the numerous Cistercian charges was in the form of what has become known as Letter 28. It is inscribed, affectionately, to Bernard himself, who is referred to as "dearest brother." From this warm tone it has been argued that the letter was never intended to be a riposte to the *Apologia*, but may actually have preceded it, in which case the roles are reversed and Peter becomes the prosecutor and Bernard the defender. What is most likely is that in the prevailing climate of accusation and counteraccusation, both Bernard's *Apologia* and Peter's Letter 28 were manifestoes intended for public consumption, independent of one another, designed to state a case to the wider world and to rally support.

Peter certainly intended his letter to be in effect a treatise, a statement of his faith and his beliefs. It must have been disseminated widely, since it appears in no fewer than seventeen surviving manuscripts. It runs to almost fifty pages, and for a mild-mannered scholar it is at times surprisingly abrasive in tone. He clearly feels hounded by repeated Cistercian attacks, and is determined to deliver a stinging counterattack. He begins with an apology for what has apparently been a lengthy delay in writing. His reasons are cryptic, but it is clear what he means. He speaks of "the great interval of lands" and "the grave bitterness of the affairs and tribulations that afflict us." The latter reference must be to the invasion of the abbey by the former Abbot Pons in 1125 and his subsequent trial and condemnation in Rome, with Peter in attendance. The "great interval of lands" may refer to the fact that while in Rome Peter was struck down with malaria and spent the next six months convalescing back in France at the monastery of Sauxillanges, with which his family enjoyed close family ties.

The main substance of his "treatise" was a vigorous defense of monasticism as had been practiced at Cluny for more than two hundred years. His was the voice of tradition, of wisdom, and of experience. By implication he suggests that the Cistercians possessed a view of the Christian life that was altogether too rigid and narrow. Furthermore it was one that lacked the quality of *caritas*, by which he seems to have meant a blend of "love" and "charity." This, he maintained, was the principle that lay at the very heart of St. Benedict's Rule, and without which the monastic life

would become heartless and inhumane. It was essential, so Peter argued in his letter, that the principle of *caritas* should always guide a monk's interpretation of the Rule, which in all matters ought to be applied with moderation and discretion, with an understanding that times and conditions of life do change, and that the daily routine of a Christian must be prepared to adapt accordingly.

For all its rhetoric and occasional bluster, Peter's defense of Cluny was a civilized and well-reasoned polemic. The principle of *caritas* was to remain a guiding light in Peter's life; it showed itself in a constant generosity of spirit, in an ability to set aside dogma in favor of human needs, together with a rare understanding of the complexity of human nature, interwoven as it was with weaknesses and self-contradictions. Here lay the true meaning of *caritas* as he understood it.

As the years progressed, Peter's relationship with Bernard grew less embattled. To a large extent this was because internal matters to do with monastic life, and wrangles about interpretations of the Rule, were by now occupying less and less of Bernard's time. He had come to stride the European stage, consorting with popes and princes, and engaging himself in larger concerns.

In 1146 Bernard was persuaded by the pope and King Louis VII of France to promote the cause of a Second Crusade to come to the aid of the Christian communities in the biblical lands and Asia Minor. In 1144 the principality of Edessa, one of the easternmost Christian territories of Mesopotamia and captured during the First Crusade, had been retaken from its Christian occupiers by Imad–ed–Din, the prince of Mosul. To rally support for a punitive reconquest and a further onslaught on Islam Bernard chose his favorite vehicle, which was the sermon. And as the setting for it he selected one of the greatest religious shrines in all of France, the abbey church of Vézelay in northwest Burgundy, where the body of Mary Magdalene was claimed to be kept, and which was one of the major starting points in France for the pilgrimage to Santiago. He decided to deliver his sermon not within the church itself but on the northern slope of the hill on which it was built. His chosen site was much like a natural amphitheater, with the church forming a dramatic backcloth. It was the 31st of March, 1146.

Bernard was a brilliant orator, and this was by all accounts a stirring and memorable occasion. Moreover it had been eagerly anticipated; the great man's words were guaranteed to draw the crowds from every walk of life. His audience included no less than the king of France and much of his family, as well as many of the most powerful men of his day, barons and churchmen alike. We do not have any record of numbers, but it was without doubt an unqualified triumph. Support for another Crusade was overwhelming, and everywhere passions ran high.

However, they were not altogether the passions Bernard had at first imagined on that day of triumph at Vézelay. What he took to be expressions of religious fervor were in many cases far from that. Bernard was a man much too absorbed by his own lofty ideals to be a perceptive judge of human character, and, unbeknown to him, among those who responded most warmly to his rallying cry were large numbers of minor feudal lords whose enthusiasm for the forthcoming Crusade had little or nothing to do with his own motivations. Many of these knights turned out to be little more than bloodthirsty fanatics who saw their own participation in the expedition as a prime opportunity for plunder on a ruthless scale. In the words of Christopher Brooke, Bernard's words preaching the cause of the Second Crusade on that spring morning in Vézelay filled the rabble with "apocalyptic hopes and sadistic dreams."

In any event, the Second Crusade was a famous disaster, with crushing military defeats in Asia Minor and an ignominious withdrawal from Damascus. A ragtag army trudged its way back as best it could. No personal blame could be attached to Bernard for the rout; he could never have anticipated the divisive opportunism that motivated so many of the adventurers who had taken part in the enterprise he had launched. For his part Abbot Peter seems to have kept a cautious distance. His letters on the subject are guardedly sympathetic, while Bernard's own account of the fiasco, addressed to Peter, was couched in uncharacteristically humble language. "I believe," he wrote, "that the exceedingly heavy and wretched groans of the Eastern Church will have reached your ears, or rather, even the innermost chambers of your heart."

Bernard himself never lost heart, and before long was even proposing to Peter that the two of them combine their energies in promoting yet another Crusade. Once again Peter's response (Letter 164) was, not surprisingly, cautious. He did go so far as to express a qualified preparedness to go to Jerusalem himself, "provided the needs of the church which is entrusted to me permitted," he added. It is not entirely clear what he meant by such a proviso: an abbot of Cluny would hardly have required permission to do anything he wished, except perhaps from the pope. The strong likelihood was that Peter was merely being diplomatic; the idea of the abbot of Cluny taking part in a military operation against Islam would have been unthinkable to him. Peter was in any case a man of peace. His writings on Islam make it clear how profoundly opposed he was to military action of any kind. His weapon was reason—never an attribute which Bernard valued particularly highly. It may be that after the violent storms of their earlier relationship, Peter was simply anxious not to provoke another explosion from the most powerful churchman of his day.

Four years later, in 1150, the atmosphere was cordial enough for Bernard to visit Cluny for Christmas—rather surprisingly, it might seem, in view of the torrents of criticism he had previously aimed at the abbey. Bernard seems to have mellowed with age, and a charter drawn up by Peter the Venerable echoes the tone of warm friendship that now prevailed, as well as demonstrating once again his own gifts as a diplomat: "Nothing suits our person and our church better than to foster gently under the bond of love the other orders which are everywhere joined to us and ours, and we wish to conserve in all ways especially those who come from the Cistercian order and particularly the house of Clairvaux, and its abbot who is most dear to us." (If ever there was a charm campaign within the ancient walls of Cluny, this was it.) In spite of everything that had passed between them, Bernard and Peter were to remain friends.

Two years after the Christmas visit (and just one year before Bernard's death), Peter found himself required to undertake a journey to Italy in midwinter. The precise reasons for the visit are unclear, but the return journey over the mountains in early spring provoked a document that touchingly illuminates aspects of Peter's nature so rarely apparent in his formal writings, in particular his physical courage and a self-deprecating gentleness. By now he was approaching sixty, and it was his last recorded letter (Letter 192):

> In the frozen Alps the peaks all around us were condemned to perpetual snow. . . . I myself felt more daring than usual, and endeavored to cross a certain bridge as a mounted rider, being wary of going on foot. But the tenacious mud sucked the rear feet of my mule backwards so that I almost fell forward into the abyss which lay beneath the bridge. But with the strength of God adding force to my mule, suddenly I found myself together with the beast safely and over the bridge. And so, apart from extreme fear, I escaped, having suffered nothing grave.

The letter is a precious cameo of a brave and modest man. The excesses of luxury and ornament at Cluny about which Bernard of Clairvaux was so scathing obviously never applied to foreign travel. Even the head of a vast empire, as Peter the Venerable still was, sometimes had no alternative but to cross the snowbound Alps on a humble mule.

XV.

Henry the King and Henry the Bishop

 Ever since the Norman Conquest England had been enjoying a special relationship with Cluny. Initially, under Abbot Hugh, this relationship had remained generally cool and impersonal, because of Hugh's reservations toward William the Conqueror as something of an upstart. By the time Peter the Venerable became abbot, Cluny had already acquired a more open and less demanding supporter in William's youngest son, Henry, who had become King Henry I in 1100. An English royal charter drawn up by Henry reads, "Let it be known that I have received into my hand and custody and protection the abbey of Cluny." Peter the Venerable, for his part, wrote, "Among all the kings of the Latin West, who for the last three hundred years have testified their affection for the church at Cluny . . . Henry, king of the English and duke of Normandy, has surpassed all others in his gifts and shown more than an ordinary share of love and attachment to us. It was he who perfected that grand basilica. . . exceeding all other known churches in the Christian world in its construction and beauty."

The particular "love and attachment" Peter was referring to was doubtless Henry's preparedness to pay the entire costs of rebuilding the great abbey church roof after it had collapsed in the year 1125.

An unexpected bonus, which no one could have been aware of at the time, was that the "grand basilica" now possessed a novel architectural feature that was soon to become a spectacular ingredient in European cathedral building over the centuries to come—the flying buttress. Doubtless the earlier collapse of the roof had necessitated something drastic in the course of rebuilding. Like most architectural inventions this one remains anonymous, though possibly some master mason once gazed up at a church wall that was in imminent danger of collapsing under the pressure of the roof and realized that the strongest way of securing it was by means of a stone support that stood free of the main structure and then "flew" upwards to attach itself to the building at an angle higher up—so providing far more powerful support than any conventional vertical buttress.

As with so many innovations, both architectural and artistic, that were once embodied in the great church of Cluny III, this one survives only in the sparse contemporary accounts that we have of the place, and in the occasional drawing made prior to its destruction. One such drawing in particular, made in the year 1617 by the Jesuit Father Martellange, clearly shows the flying buttresses supporting the nave wall of the church along its entire length.

King Henry's personal life was to have a powerful bearing on the fortunes of Cluny. He was a shrewd political tactician with the priceless gift of knowing how to keep one step ahead of his rivals— in particular his brother Robert II (Robert Curthose), duke of Normandy. Robert had a far sounder claim to the throne of England than Henry, but at the time when his elder brother King William II (William Rufus) was killed in 1100 Henry was conveniently close to the English capital, Winchester, and saw to it that he was crowned there as quickly as possible. Meanwhile Robert Curthose was still far away, returning from the First Crusade.

Henry promptly reinforced his insecure position as king of England by marrying a princess from an ancient Anglo-Saxon royal line—Matilda, the daughter of the king of Scotland. Henry's own connection with Cluny seems to have been greatly strengthened by his marriage to Matilda. Between them, as Peter the Venerable acknowledged with profound gratitude, they took over from the Spanish kings as the principal benefactors of the abbey. In addition to his decisive contribution to the roof repair of the abbey church Henry made other valuable gifts both to Cluny itself and to its eldest daughter house a short distance away, the priory of La Charité-sur-Loire. Matilda made her own contribution to the new abbey church in spectacular style—a giant seven-branched candelabrum which was an imaginary replica of the one in the Tabernacle described in the book of Exodus. A contemporary chronicler gave an account of it as being made of copper gilt and set with crystals and "beryls," and with a stem eighteen feet in height. Not surprisingly Bernard of Clairvaux duly voiced his contempt. "The church is adorned with crowns of light—nay, with lusters like cart wheels," he observed acidly, "girt all round with lamps, but no less brilliant are the precious stones that stud them. Moreover we see candelabra standing like trees of massive bronze, fashioned with marvelous subtlety of art, and glistening no less brightly with gems than with the lights they carry. What, think you, is the purpose of all this?"

Meanwhile King Henry continued to shower favors on Cluny. He appears to have been a monarch considerably more pious in public than he was in private; Henry is reputed to have fathered twenty illegitimate children, but also managed to sire two legitimate offspring. One of these was his son and heir, William, though by the time Peter became abbot of Cluny William was already dead, drowned along with many other members of the royal household when his ship, known as the *White Ship*, foundered and sank shortly after leaving the Norman port of Barfleur in November 1120. A year later King Henry founded Reading Abbey, motivated largely by the tragic death of his son. Henry laid the foundation stone himself, and wrote to Cluny requesting that he be sent as many monks as could be spared in order to help establish the new abbey on Cluniac lines. His plan was to supplement these with other monks drawn from Lewes Priory, which had been founded under the aegis of his father, William the Conqueror.

Henry's other legitimate offspring was a daughter who shared her mother's name, Matilda. Henry negotiated a marriage between her and the Holy Roman Emperor Henry V; then, after the emperor's early death in 1125, he arranged her second marriage to the youthful Geoffrey Plantagenet, heir to the count of Anjou (to whom she was to bear a son who became the first Plantagenet king of England, Henry II). It was his daughter Matilda who cemented Henry's personal link with Cluny even more strongly. She was a deeply pious lady whose principal contribution to the new abbey church was the gift of a set of bells that were transported from England where they had been cast—and which survived at Cluny until the final pillage of the abbey in the aftermath of the French Revolution. In 1125, recently widowed, she took herself to Santiago de Compostela as a pilgrim (certainly with a substantial retinue); and it was during her stay in Santiago that she was presented with a gift that was to become a potent symbol of the link between Cluny and England. The gift was a holy relic of very special importance to medieval believers—one of the hands of the apostle St. James the Greater. After her return to England she presented her father with the hand of the apostle, and Henry promptly entrusted the revered relic to the care of the new abbey at Reading.

A letter from the king to the abbot survives: "Henry, King of England and Duke of Normandy, to the Abbot and Convent of Reading, greeting. Know ye that the glorious hand of the blessed James the Apostle, which Empress Matilda, my daughter, gave me… I, at her request, send to you and grant for ever to the Church of Reading…." (Henry's reference to himself as Duke of Normandy is pertinent. The man who legally held that title was actually his elder brother Robert Curthose, whom Henry had defeated in battle and proceeded to hold in prison for the remainder of his life.)

Reading Abbey was founded by one Henry and destroyed in 1539 by another—Henry VIII. In the centuries between it became the most important Cluniac link with England, more so even than Lewes Priory, though it always remained independent of Cluny's direct authority while continuing to observe the abbey's rules and practices.

One reason for the elevated status of Reading Abbey was the lavishness of its royal endowment. More important still was the wealth of the relics it held. The abbey, like so many other Cluniac churches, was constructed with a generous ambulatory so that pilgrims could circulate round and behind the high altar on feast days in order to appreciate the precious relics on view. And what a collection lay before them. The celebrated hand of St. James may have been the principal object of reverence, but there were others not far behind: a piece of Christ's shoe, a phial containing blood from his side, some hair and garments of the Virgin Mary, the robe of Doubting Thomas, a tooth of St. Luke, bits of Aaron's rod, a fragment of the rock which Moses struck, a piece of the Holy Cross, and—in the eyes of the pilgrims of lesser worth—various fingers belonging to minor Christian martyrs.

The impact of Cluny on England during this period was probably most decisive in the field of architecture. It is necessary to use the word "probably" since the building likely to have exerted the greatest influence on Norman England—the abbey church Cluny III—scarcely exists. Plans of that great church, and almost certainly drawings, are known to have been brought to England, besides which its reputation as the greatest church in Christian Europe would have quickened the imagination of church builders both in Normandy and across the Channel. The middle decades of the twelfth century, more or less coinciding with the abbacy of Peter the Venerable, were the years during which Norman culture in England enjoyed a remarkable flowering. This was the period when many of the finest Norman cathedrals were under construction, among them Canterbury, Ely, Durham, Norwich, Peterborough, and Rochester.

In 1126 Henry I made an appointment in England that was to have a dynamic effect on the fortunes of Cluny for the next fifty years. Henry's young nephew, the son of the Conqueror's daughter Adèle, had become a monk at Cluny—maybe a surprising decision for a scion of a royal house, but then he was no ordinary young man. His name was Henry of Blois, his father having been the count of Blois. For how long Henry remained at Cluny is unclear, but he must have returned to England still relatively young, in anticipation of higher things. King Henry proceeded to appoint his nephew to not just one, but two prestigious offices in the English church. First he made him abbot of Glastonbury, then the wealthiest religious house in the land; more important still, three years later he appointed him bishop of Winchester, which was the richest bishopric in England, a post Henry proceeded to hold for forty-two years. From being a monk sworn to poverty and the cloistered life, he became within just a few years a figure of colossal wealth and power.

Henry of Blois is one of the most colorful figures in medieval England, and in some respects one of the most outrageous. He was not, to put it mildly, a humble monk by nature. He was a person of restless energy, a man of action, a military figure, a statesman and politician, a formidable administrator and a lavish patron of the arts. He was also the brother of the man who was to usurp the English throne in 1135 after the death of King Henry I—Stephen; and it was as Stephen's right-hand man that he was to become one of the most powerful men in the country. Changing loyalties was never one of his problems. Somewhere in the midst of all these activities he also carved out a career as a churchman. In fact, as a papal legate he came to occupy a position within the English church almost equal in importance to that of the archbishop of Canterbury.

As bishop of Winchester he lost no time before demonstrating the affection and loyalty he continued to feel for Cluny. Around the year 1130 he donated the huge sum of seven thousand pieces of silver, just at the time when Abbot Peter was struggling to balance the abbey's books. He also paid for a large crucifix to be mounted by the high altar, with the figure of Christ in silver gilt complete with a crown—not of thorns, but of gold.

Bernard's reaction to this latest Cluniac excess is not hard to guess. But then few churchmen can ever have been further apart both in character and lifestyle than Bernard of Clairvaux and Henry of Blois. They were both astute politicians, but there the similarities ended. To Bernard the bishop was simply "that whore of Winchester." And in 1136 it was largely his open hostility that denied Henry of Blois the archbishopric of Canterbury.

In the same year it was at Henry's personal invitation that Peter the Venerable made a tour of religious houses in England, where by all accounts he was treated royally wherever he went. The two men had by now become close friends. Even though Peter was a generous and forgiving man it seems likely that his kindness must at times have been tested to the full whenever his noble patron behaved like a feudal barbarian. Once, in a fit of tyrannical rage Henry deliberately burned much of his city of Winchester to the ground along with its monastery and nunnery. Nonetheless, Peter seems to have been able to preserve the larger picture of the man, and continued to see much good in him.

Henry for his part always managed somehow to keep a precarious balance between being a military bishop, an international statesman, and a Cluniac monk. All his life he showed himself to be adept at appearing to do the right thing even when blatantly doing the opposite. A blend of wealth, charm, and a bullying persuasiveness generally brought him whatever he wanted. He was also brilliant at display: he took pains to follow his cousin Matilda's example in making the prescribed pilgrimage to Santiago de Compostela, doubtless with an even larger retinue. For a former Cluniac monk the journey would have been particularly rewarding, as he would have seen for himself the impressive chain of Cluniac monasteries that serviced the Spanish pilgrim road, and this experience would have strengthened his respect for the abbey that, after all, had been his school and his spiritual home.

The journey may also have contributed to the most surprising of all the decisions taken by this brilliant and wayward medieval churchman. At the age of sixty Henry went into self-exile and retired to Cluny. This was in 1156, and his friend Peter the Venerable was dying. It is tempting to see his personal affection for the old abbot as a motive for this sudden retreat from the raw political world in which he had operated so vigorously. Clearly there were other motives as well. During the years when his brother Stephen occupied the throne of England Henry of Blois was one of the key figures in the land. But Stephen had died in 1154, and power now lay with King Henry's daughter and rightful heir, Matilda, against whom Stephen had fought a long and bitter civil war to keep her from the throne. Now, by an agreement which Stephen had signed, it was Matilda's son, the young Henry of Anjou (yet another Henry), who succeeded to the English throne. He became Henry II, England's first Plantagenet king. With his brother Stephen dead the bishop now found himself out in the cold. The years of his political power and glory were suddenly eclipsed. And so at this appropriate moment Cluny offered a welcome shelter.

But no sooner had he sunk into his Burgundian retreat in the gentle valley of the Grosne than the old energy returned with a vengeance. Not for Henry of Blois, it seems, was the quiet contemplative life of liturgy and prayer; he proceeded to take on the complex economic administration of the abbey and much of the entire Cluniac order, and did so with a flair and an organizational brilliance that no one at Cluny had ever experienced. For a while at least, what had been a wounded empire became a flourishing business. In addition Henry drew on his vast personal wealth to support single-handedly the entire monastic community of Cluny, thus becoming both the abbey's banker and protector.

Henry remained at Cluny until the job was done. And then he returned to his bishopric at Winchester to become a lavish patron of a celebrated school of manuscript illumination as well as of other applied arts which flourished in the English capital under his patronage—ivory, metalwork, stone carving among them. And it was at Winchester, at the age of seventy-two, that Bishop Henry died.

XVI

Héloïse and Abelard

We hear little about women in the Cluniac world. St. Benedict had written for men, and almost all of the founders and patrons of monasteries were men, and so they tended to ignore the nuns. By the mid-eleventh century, for every four male monasteries in England there was only one nunnery, and in France the numbers were probably even more disproportionate. Monastery documents were written by men, for men, and mostly about men. But for the fact that monks had mothers and sisters it would be easy to assume that only one sex existed.

Nevertheless, women did play a prominent role within the Cluniac empire. It was Abbot Hugh who founded the first Cluniac nunnery, Marcigny, in 1055 to provide a home for his mother and sister and a group of like-minded women; and Hugh's sister Ermengarde became Marcigny's first prioress. But overall, according to Christopher Brooke, in *The Monastic World*,

> the abbots of Cluny of the eleventh century, like most of the great monastic organizers of the eleventh and twelfth centuries, were averse to nuns, arguing that they distracted monks from their proper tasks and lay difficulties and temptations at their gates. Such men set their faces sternly against the double monastery, though a few survived and a few more

were founded; small communities of nuns attached to male houses were by no means rare. The holy and importunate widow could not be held indefinitely at bay, especially if she were rich and strong of will. . . . Most of the new houses of nuns of this age and the next struggled into existence on a very modest scale; often they were small and poor, little more than depositories for daughters with moderate dowries. Sometimes even the poor houses grew to considerable wealth if they were near great cities and the dowries and legacies fell thick upon them. . . . They were commonly served by chaplains from one order or another; and it sometimes happens that the documents fail to specify to what order the nuns themselves belonged. . . . The chaplains were an essential feature of any house of nuns, since the sisters could not be in holy orders, and so could not perform the sacraments. In most houses there were a number of male officials and servants, besides the multitude of maidservants that attended any flock of well-to-do ladies. Even very poor houses must have had some menservants, to act as porters and guardians of the house.

Nothing survives of Marcigny, but a short distance to the north of Cluny are the remains of another women's monastic institution. This was the small priory of Lancharre, founded late in the eleventh century by the local lords of Brancion. The outer walls and a handsome entrance gate survive, and so does much of the priory church built mainly in the twelfth century as a smaller version of the great Lombard church of Chapaize a little over a mile away. The members of Lancharre were canonesses—women who lived according to a religious canon, or rule, but not under a lifelong vow like regular nuns. In practice they were highborn women of independent means whose vows, such as they were, certainly never included the vow of poverty. Each of the "Ladies of Lancharre," as they were known, possessed a house of her own with one or more personal servants, and in this gracious manner they pursued a life of gentility and leisure—perhaps of pleasure too, of a discreet kind—very much in the mould established later by the movement of the Beguines in parts of Germany and the Low Countries.

Strictly speaking Lancharre counted as a dependency of Cluny since the ladies ostensibly embraced the Rule of St. Benedict, or at least those parts of it that suited them. But one suspects that the strongest appeal of the place for these ladies of wealth lay less in embracing the Rule than being free from the rule of men. Generally speaking, unless they were royal or titled in their own right, women at this time had no status at all except in terms of their relation to men, whether as daughters, wives, mothers, or widows. Often the only freedom from such dependence lay in joining a religious order. In doing so women were enabled to preserve their integrity, both of body and soul; and what might appear to be a retreat from the world could become a way of wielding a certain power within it—or at least of enjoying a certain independence.

The existence of this little priory of independent women at Lancharre gives a heartening slant on what was most often a rough and masculine world. Even from the small amount we know of life within this little community we get as glimpse of a close and humane existence far removed from the rhetoric and the ideological swordplay so often indulged in by the church at large. It was also a community brought closer to us today by the portraits of several noble prioresses engraved on their respective tombstones which have survived inside the priory church. One pert and prettily dressed lady—looking far too young to be a prioress and far too young to die—could have been a perfect match for Chaucer's prioress in *The Canterbury Tales*, with her head neatly bound in a "ful semyly wympul" and an expression on her face of one who would never in her life have let any "morsel from hir lippes falle."

Not surprisingly relationships with women feature rarely in the letters of Cluny's abbots or in the official accounts of their lives. One notable exception is Peter the Venerable, and the lady with whom he corresponded with deep feeling was that tragic and heroic figure, Héloïse, the former wife and widow of the philosopher Peter Abelard. Her link with Cluny is a moving one, as well as an abiding tribute to the humanity of its last great abbot.

The marriage and parting of Héloïse and Abelard is one of the most heartrending love stories in European history, and one that has been told many times, sometimes factually, more often fancifully. As far as Cluny's involvement with them is concerned, the story of the two lovers and the subsequent events governing their lives needs to be seen within the context of the close and long-standing relationship that existed between Peter the Venerable, who protected Abelard, and the man who chose to persecute him, Bernard of Clairvaux.

Remarkably, the issue of Abelard—both his love affair with Héloïse and his "heretical" writings—never became a bone of contention between the two men. Both Bernard and Peter the Venerable seem to have taken pains to avoid addressing the subject in their letters; perhaps there were quite enough differences between them already without either man wishing to add one more.

More than a decade before Peter became abbot of Cluny in 1122, and several years before Bernard and his band of followers joined Stephen Harding's monastery at Citeaux, the young Peter

Abelard had become the most celebrated scholar and religious teacher in France. He was the intellectual colossus of his day, contributing greatly to making Paris the first full-fledged university north of the Alps. Abelard himself was a Breton, the son of a nobleman from near Nantes, who had abandoned the life of a feudal baron and the prospect of a glittering military career in order to study philosophy in Paris. He proceeded to set up his own school not far away, at Melun, and subsequently at Corbeil.

Back in Paris he acquired widespread fame as a dialectician, becoming the leading exponent of Aristotelian logic. His teaching platform was the secular post he was awarded at the cathedral of Notre Dame—that of *Magister scholarum*. For convenience he took lodgings in the cathedral precinct at the house of one of the canons by the name of Fulbert. Abelard was now a man in his late thirties, unmarried and with no domestic ties. Canon Fulbert was no doubt honored to have one of the most celebrated men of his day under his roof, and duly approached Abelard to enquire if he would be prepared to become the private tutor of his young niece. She was his sister's daughter, a clever and ambitious young woman of about twenty by the name of Héloïse, who had come to live in her uncle's house in order to further her education in Paris. Abelard duly accepted Fulbert's proposal.

For a while the relationship appears to have been nothing more than that of tutor and pupil. On the other hand the tutor was a man of powerful intellect and personality, while the pupil was beautiful and extremely bright. Both were unattached. Abelard had taken no religious vows. What was more, they were living in the same house, and often found themselves alone. Precisely when and how the relationship changed to being a love affair we know only from Abelard's autobiography, written some fifteen years later as a long confessional in the form of an open letter. According to him the affair began as a straightforward seduction on his part. Subsequently it became a whirlwind that swept up both of them. Abelard wrote her love poems and set them to music, as well as passionate love letters. They became helplessly and erotically in love. "Under the pretence of lessons we abandoned ourselves to our love," Abelard wrote. "My hands strayed more often over her breasts than over the pages of her books."

With hindsight he could sometimes be more circumspect about the relationship. "Luck always makes fools conceited," he observed. "Worldly security slackens the power of the intellect and easily destroys it through the temptations of the flesh. I already considered myself to be the only philosopher left in the world, and no longer feared to be troubled by anyone."

Abelard's unwillingness to be "troubled by anyone" had its inevitable consequence. Héloïse became pregnant. Abelard promptly abducted her from Canon Fulbert's house and took her, disguised as a man, to his native Brittany. Here she stayed with his sister and gave birth to a son (curiously named Astrolabe). Shortly afterwards Abelard and Héloïse secretly married, whereupon at Abelard's insistence Héloïse retired to a convent at Argenteuil, outside Paris, apparently to escape the fury of her uncle, while Abelard returned to the city seemingly unabashed, to find that he had now lost his teaching post at Notre Dame.

In a short time Fulbert's fury was unleashed on Abelard. The canon succeeded in bribing two of Abelard's servants to leave their master's door unlocked at night. Fulbert's hired ruffians then proceeded to enter his room while Abelard slept and castrated him.

Obviously neither Cluny nor Clairvaux played any part whatsoever in any of these happenings. The intimate involvement of both parties comes some time later, as a direct result of what followed.

The immediate outcome of the brutal attack was that Abelard decided to retreat into the monastic life at the royal abbey of Saint-Denis, outside Paris. As for Héloïse, Abelard insisted against her wishes that she become a nun at the Argenteuil convent where she was staying. Then, after the convent dispersed, Abelard gave her a property between Paris and Troyes on which she founded a community of nuns known as the Paraclete (Le Paraclet). Héloïse herself became its first abbess, and remained there for the rest of her long life.

Why Abelard behaved as he did, rejecting his wife and son in favor of a monastic life, has been debated over and over again. It was certainly not forced upon him. He was legally married. He had money, fame, and a social position. He could have withdrawn from public life if he chose, to live quietly with his family. His philosophical studies did not necessitate taking holy orders. But perhaps these are modern concepts. In medieval Christendom the monastic life was frequently a haven for those whom the ugly world had wounded. A monastery was the universal protector, the healing balm, a glimpse of heaven on earth. We can only assume that shame, remorse, and shock at what had been inflicted on him drove all thoughts of love and domesticity from Abelard's mind, causing him to repudiate everything that had once passed between him and

Héloïse—at least for a long while; many years later he sent Héloïse books of hymns he had composed, and together they compiled a collection of their old love letters. For the two of them it was a belated reliving of their golden days. "The lovers' pleasures which we enjoyed together were so sweet to me that they can never displease me," Héloïse wrote to Abelard after a gap of twelve years, "I ought to deplore what we did, but I sigh only for what we have lost."

Meanwhile Abelard threw himself back into his religious studies, and into teaching. His chosen area of work consisted of systematically applying principles of logical analysis to a broad range of Christian dogma, in the course of which he found himself repeatedly challenging theological orthodoxy and as a result incurring the wrath of the established church. Building on what he had learnt from a careful study of the Greek philosophers and of Roman law, he insisted loudly that the function of dialectics was to draw a distinction between those aspects of theology which rang true and those that rang false. Church dogma, he maintained, needed to relate to what we know and understand in this world, and not be accepted blindly on the strength of oft-quoted authorities which were themselves often suspect. He went so far as to compose treatises for the benefit of his students offering guidelines as to how they should approach the numerous inconsistencies to be found in official Church teaching. And as if this was not enough provocation, he wrote the first version of his book, *Theologia*, in which he threw down an even weightier challenge to orthodoxy by offering a dialectical analysis of the mysteries of God and of the Trinity. He also openly praised the "pagan" philosophers of classical antiquity, suggesting that through the application of reason they had succeeded in anticipating many aspects of the Christian faith.

This was altogether too much and an unacceptable provocation to the church hierarchy. Before the contribution of Thomas Aquinas a century later, the notion that Christianity might owe a crucial debt to "pagan" philosophers was unthinkable to traditional theologians. Accordingly the *Theologia* was condemned as heretical and formally burned, and its author placed temporarily under house arrest.

By now Abelard's unwavering intellectual self-confidence was winning him a host of admirers among his students, but alarm was beginning to spread very quickly indeed within the established church. Someone had to be found to pull Abelard down. Only one person in France was seen to possess sufficient authority and influence within the hierarchy to undertake such a task, and that was the most influential figure in Christian Europe at the time— Bernard of Clairvaux. It was well known that Bernard's views on religious faith were diametrically opposed to those of Abelard. His was a simple and mystical faith unencumbered by intellectual considerations. Inevitably then, the moment Bernard undertook to confront Abelard a clash between the two became unavoidable.

We can only guess what Peter the Venerable's views were at this stage as he listened to the distant sounds of battle from the Burgundy countryside. As a fellow scholar and classicist he would have felt deep sympathy with many of Abelard's opinions, particularly in his admiration for the Greek philosophers, Aristotle above all. But equally, as a cautious man, a diplomat and a man of peace, he would have disapproved strongly of Abelard's stance in deliberately provoking attack by pouring scorn on what were still considered to be fundamental tenets of the Christian faith. The search for truth, he believed, should not be conducted with belligerence.

There can be no doubt that Abelard was asking for trouble, and that he believed his superior intellect automatically rendered him invulnerable to attack; he assumed that reason was bound to win the day. The weakness of his position was a naive inability to grasp that not everyone in authority within the church shared his belief in the supremacy of reason. Bernard, for one, most certainly did not.

Bernard's denunciation of Abelard became another crusade. He referred to his opponent as a "dragon" and a "snake," the latter being a reference to the serpent in the Garden of Eden, a clear allusion to Abelard's physical relationship with Héloïse, which would have disgusted Bernard. But his fundamental quarrel with the philosopher lay in Abelard's application of logical analysis to matters of religious faith. Bernard argued passionately that the mysteries of God were unique and could only be degraded by use of reason; therefore the pagan Greek philosophers had nothing whatsoever to offer a Christian except knowledge for the sake of knowledge, which was of no value in matters of faith. One seeks God, he wrote, "not through scandalous curiosity. . . . We discover [God] with greater facility through prayer than through disputation." Faith for Bernard was a mystical experience that could overrule all reason, and was therefore impregnable to all argument.

Not surprisingly he was determined to see Abelard condemned as a heretic, and set about using all his considerable influence with church leaders to bring this about. Matters came to a head at a church council convened in June 1140 in the cathedral of Sens, southeast of Paris, largely at Bernard's insistence. Bernard refused to debate with Abelard directly, doubtless sensing he would come off worse. Instead he offered no fewer than nineteen propositions to prove that Abelard was a heretic, and made a direct appeal to Pope Innocent II to that effect. It is not entirely clear whether the way the Sens council was operated gave Abelard no opportunity to present his case, or whether he contemptuously decided not to do so since Bernard consistently refused to lock horns with him. In either case the outcome was the same: one month later, on July 16, the pope responded to Bernard's appeal with two letters, one addressed to the archbishop of Sens and the other to Bernard himself, duly condemning Abelard as a heretic.

It would have been gratifying had the pope shown himself to be a broader-minded man able to take a more conciliatory view of

Bernard's bludgeoning approach. But Pope Innocent, along with most of the leading churchmen of his day, was too much in awe of the formidable abbot of Clairvaux, and simply did as he was told. As a result all Abelard's followers were excommunicated, and Abelard himself ordered to be placed in the custody of a monastery. Meanwhile all his books were to be burned, the pope himself undertaking to set up a stake at St. Peter's in Rome for that specific purpose. Abelard had been convicted without a hearing and without a trial. Bernard had won, not by argument, but by personal influence.

The final chapter of Abelard's life is a sad one. His first intention following the papal condemnation was to take himself to Rome in order to present his case personally to the pope. But he was by now in his sixties and a sick man. His journey took him only as far as Cluny where Peter the Venerable welcomed him and took care of him. And at Cluny Abelard began to compose his defense of the nineteen charges that had been brought against him. Even in ill-health his self-confidence remained intact, and he continued to believe that his answers to the charges would win the day in Rome and result inevitably in the literary demolition of Bernard.

It was a disingenuous hope. His health also worsened. The likelihood of Abelard being strong enough to make the journey to Rome lessened by the day. Meanwhile Peter the Venerable undertook to keep the pope informed of Abelard's condition, and asked permission to keep the sick man in the protection of a Cluny for the remainder of his life—a request to which the pope agreed. Peter, ever the diplomat, also took the initiative of discreetly negotiating a meeting of reconciliation between the two adversaries, Bernard and Abelard. The suggestion seems to have been made indirectly to Bernard, no doubt to avoid the risk of yet another clash of opinions between the two men. In any event, both parties agreed. It is unclear whether Abelard made the journey to

Clairvaux or perhaps to some neutral place nearby. In any case it seems that Bernard, witnessing Abelard's condition, softened his stance towards the philosopher, and as a result the two men belatedly made their peace. *Et factunt est ita* was Bernard's abrupt verdict. "And it was done."

That was all. The battle was over. Maybe Abelard was by now too exhausted to fight any longer. It may also have been the effect of Peter's lifelong belief in *caritas* which enabled the two adversaries to lay down their arms. It was a final triumph for the man of peace. "He went and came back," Peter wrote to the pope, "and on his return told us he had made his peace with Bernard and that their previous differences were settled."

Abelard was approaching death. Peter moved him to the nearby monastery of St. Marcel, outside Chalon-sur-Saône, where the climate was deemed to be more favorable. And it was here that Abelard died, in April 1142, one and a half years after he had taken refuge at Cluny.

It could all have ended there—a chapter closed. But Peter chose otherwise. He began a correspondence with Héloïse of a deeply moving kind, referring to her as Abelard's wife and offering her an account of her husband's life as he had witnessed it. "In the last years of his life Providence sent him to Cluny," he wrote, "and in doing so enriched this place in his person with a gift more precious than any gold or topaz. . . . And so Master Peter ended his days. He was known all over the world for his unique mastery of knowledge. . . . If I am not mistaken, I remember having seen no person to compare with him in humility." He went on to assure her that Christ would keep Abelard for her, and that at the Second Coming of the Lord God would return him to her.

At Héloïse's request Abelard's body was taken to her convent of the Paraclete. Remarkably Peter the Venerable made the significant gesture of accompanying it personally. What seems extraordinary is that the head of a prominent monastic order was thus seen to be openly following the coffin of a condemned heretic. Nothing tells us more eloquently than this courageous act where Peter stood in relation to the dispute between Bernard and Abelard.

At the Paraclete he met Héloïse for the first time. It was nearly thirty years since her love affair with Abelard, and she was now a woman in her late forties. We have no idea how their meeting proceeded, except that Peter agreed to send her his absolution for Abelard. This reached her in the form of a sealed charter which she duly hung on her husband's tomb. Peter also offered to compose an epitaph for Abelard, and in this he voiced surprisingly strong disapproval of the way in which Bernard had sought the condemnation of the philosopher. Peter himself described Abelard unreservedly as "the Socrates of the Gauls, the great Plato of the West, our Aristotle."

This ruling principle of Peter's abbacy at Cluny, *caritas*, was a humanity and generosity of mind which manifested itself most obviously in Peter's behavior towards both Abelard and Héloïse, but the spirit of *caritas* flowed into other areas of monastic life as well. It may be no accident that it was during Peter's years as abbot that some of the finest works of art in medieval Europe were produced under the extended umbrella of Cluny, in particular the carvings in the abbey church of Vézelay—where Peter's brother held the post of abbot—and the even greater carvings for the cathedral at Autun, carried out by one of the first medieval sculptors we can actually identify, the man who signed himself in stone over the cathedral door as—*Gislebertus*.

XVII.

Genius in Stone

We are in pursuit of a shadow—a long shadow that stretches out from those dancing and fluttering figures representing the seasons of the year and the eight tones of Gregorian chant which are now displayed in Cluny's Musée du Farinier, but which once crowned the columns half-encircling the choir of the abbey church.

Together with the few fragments of the lost tympanum over the west portal of the church excavated in the 1950s by Kenneth Conant, these carvings are virtually all the sculpture that survives from Cluny III. Yet they are enough to demonstrate that here was the true source, the fountainhead, from which emerged some of the finest achievements in sacred art of the entire Middle Ages. It was here in Cluny that Romanesque sculpture emerged from being a crude instrument of church doctrine and grotesquerie to become a vehicle for the most intense human passions and human dreams.

Two sculptural ensembles in particular, neither of them very far from Cluny, owe their inspiration primarily to this place. They are the carved portals and capitals of two of the finest examples of Romanesque architecture in Burgundy, and indeed in all of Europe—the former abbey church of Mary Magdalene at Vézelay, and the cathedral of St. Lazare at Autun. The long shadow of Cluny extends to the artists of genius who worked on these two churches, and one of them, for almost the first time in the anonymous world of medieval workshops, we can actually identify by name: Gislebertus, or Gilbert.

The subject of Gislebertus, and what he did or did not personally carve, has been an academic minefield ever since a layer of eighteenth-century plaster was removed from the tympanum of the Last Judgment above the west door of Autun cathedral, and his name was suddenly revealed boldly inscribed in stone beneath the feet of Christ in Majesty: *Gislebertus hoc fecit*, "Gislebertus made this."

At least there has never been any argument about the extent of his contribution at Autun. The west tympanum of the cathedral was his and his alone, and he said so proudly. What is more, the local bishop and church authorities who commissioned him must have been very proud of his work, too, or they would never have permitted their master sculptor to sign his name so extravagantly in proximity to the Son of God. It was unprecedented, and a sign of the respect in which he was held.

The task of carving the numerous panels of the tympanum, along with a large amount of other work in the cathedral, took Gislebertus approximately ten years, from about 1125 to 1135. The building of the new cathedral had begun some years earlier, about 1120. The circumstances were somewhat bizarre, though hardly unusual for the times: Autun had been presented with what were deemed to be the remains of Lazarus, the friend of Christ whom he had raised from the dead, and who was then supposed to have voyaged to Gaul, along with his sisters Mary Magdalene and Martha, where he became the first bishop of Marseille before eventually being martyred.

The improbability of this tale did not apparently tax the credulity of twelfth-century men and women in Burgundy. The cult of holy relics was at its zenith, and relics of this status were the most lucrative investment any church could make. Accordingly a new church needed to be built in Autun in order to house the supposed remains of Lazarus, as well as to accommodate the scores of pilgrims, rich and poor, who would very soon flock to Autun to revere them.

To begin with, it was the intention of the local bishop, Etienne, who was a friend and staunch admirer of Cluny, to model his new cathedral on the magnificent new abbey church there. And for the next four or five years building work seems to have progressed along these lines, with a modest amount of decorative carving being carried out, none of it of any special note.

But at this moment something dramatic occurred which was to alter the whole character of the project. After the roof over the nave of Cluny's abbey church had collapsed in 1125, the bishop appears to have abandoned the idea of copying Cluny, and to have insisted instead on a completely fresh design, one that was to be drawn up by—presumably—a fresh architect. Who he was we have no idea, but his appointment coincided with a decision to commission a new master sculptor who would be responsible for the sculptural work throughout the entire church. This bold change of plan suggests that Bishop Etienne was a forceful man, with very positive ideas about the kind of talent he wished to employ. Suddenly, from rather conservative beginnings the whole building operation at Autun seems to have acquired a new and dynamic sense of purpose.

For any sculptor this was clearly a highly prestigious commission. And the fact that it was offered to Gislebertus, and that he was to undertake the work personally rather than share it out among an anonymous team of carvers, suggests that he must already have been an artist with a high and very special reputation, someone the bishop and authorities of Autun valued and had singled out for his individual skills.

So, where could Gislebertus have acquired those skills which gave him such a high reputation, and where could the church elders at Autun have been able to see evidence of them? Certainly not at Autun itself, which at that date possessed no workshop of any standing, nor any history of high artistic achievement of any kind— at least not since the departure of the Romans many centuries earlier.

The probable answer is that Gislebertus had received his training at Cluny, and that outstanding examples of his work might have been visible there for Bishop Etienne and his colleagues to see and admire.

But here is where scholarly debate begins to intensify, and other arguments are presented. It needs to be said that there are no contemporary records of any kind relating to Gislebertus. If it were not for that one bold signature above the cathedral door at Autun we would not even know his name. Any association with places other than Autun, and with other works of sculpture, must be entirely conjectural, on the basis of stylistic comparison alone.

Inevitably there is little agreement here. The leading proponent of the view than Gislebertus was already a master craftsman at Cluny before working at Autun was the late George Zarnecki, who in 1961 also bore the credentials of being the coauthor of the first and (to date) only book in English on Gislebertus, his collaborator being a local historian and churchman, the Abbé Grivot. In Zarnecki's view, the sculptor not only trained at Cluny but subsequently "took an active and even prominent part in the work of decorating the Cluny abbey church." Several of the surviving fragments of carving have been attributed to him by a number of scholars, notably the Expulsion from Paradise capital in the Musée du Farinier and two fragments of the western portal excavated in the 1950s, namely the bearded heads of two of the twenty-four elders of the Apocalypse, now preserved in the Musée d'Art et d'Archéologie at Cluny.

If these are truly by the hand of Gislebertus, then—since only a minute percentage of the original carvings for the abbey church survive—the probability is that he must have executed much else besides. He is likely therefore to have been, claimed Zarnecki, one of the chief assistants to the master mason in charge of the Cluny workshop, all of which would explain why his reputation was as high as it was, and why he was awarded such a prestigious commission at Autun.

Evidence to support this view rests on direct comparison. One of the most striking characteristics of Gislebertus's style, visible over and over again in the tympanum at Autun and on many of the fifty or more capitals he carved for the cathedral, is the way he used a fine chisel to pick out in close parallel lines the folds and movement of drapery, so giving the human form an air of lightness as if his figures were windblown and never still. Under his touch cold stone comes to warm life, and the figures carved in it seem about to free themselves from its constraints. And it is here that the link between Cluny and Autun is unmistakable. One of the capitals carved by Gislebertus for the nave of Autun depicts the fourth tone of Gregorian chant. This is symbolized by the figure of a musician who is ringing a line of bells suspended from a rod he carries on his shoulder. In typical fashion the musician's garments swirl around him as he appears to be walking while he rings the bells.

The carving is pure Gislebertus. At the same time it also turns out to be a free adaptation of one of those surviving capitals that once half-encircled the choir of the Cluny church. But it is unlikely that Gislebertus also carved the original scene, given the probable date.

But something is still missing here, and a further argument begins to emerge. To the north of Autun lies the former abbey church of Vézelay. It is the largest Romanesque church surviving in France, and its carved tympanum remains one of the wonders of the world. Vézelay was hugely renowned as a pilgrim center on account of its claim—fraudulent as it turned out—to be in possession of the body of Mary Magdalene. The abbey itself later fell into decay and was finally razed to the ground during the French Revolution. But a large number of carved fragments have been painstakingly assembled in the local Musée Lapidaire, and meticulously catalogued under the direction of the English scholar Neil Stratford. One of these fragments is part of a triangular gable, badly damaged, but what remains of the principal figure includes a flow of drapery whose folds have been carved rhythmically in a series of swirling parallel lines in exactly the way costume is represented over and over again at Autun.

Along with two further fragments in the museum that display the same characteristics, Zarnecki believed that "these were carved by Gislebertus himself." A bold hypothesis. He went on to propose a time frame—which became another issue of heated scholarly dispute.

In June 1120 a devastating fire had broken out at Vézelay, completely destroying the abbey church and killing more than one thousand pilgrims who were attending a service there, so it is said. Vézelay's abbot at the time of this disaster was a certain Renaud de Semur, a nephew of the former Abbot Hugh. And when he set a massive rebuilding program in motion for Vézelay the man he appointed to oversee the work of the stone masons was a young Cluniac monk by the name of Pierre de Montboissier. Two years later this man was elected to the office of abbot of Cluny itself—the person we have come to know as Peter the Venerable.

The many strands linking Vézelay intimately to Cluny make it likely that after the disastrous fire of 1120 it was to Cluny that

Abbot Renaud appealed for skilled masons and sculptors to enable him to rebuild his burnt-out shell of a church. And in view of the stylistic similarities between carvings at Cluny, Autun, and Vézelay, there is the likelihood that one of these craftsmen was the young Gislebertus. In other words, so Zarnecki's theory runs, after receiving his training at Cluny, then rising to become a chief assistant to the master mason, Gislebertus left the abbey to join a new team working on the rebuilding of Vézelay, until he was summoned some five years later to be the artistic overlord at Autun, around the year 1125. This is a tangled tale—hypothesis piled upon hypothesis. But what remains beyond doubt is that Gislebertus was regarded as someone who was entirely special.

Autun was Caesar Augustus's city, *Augustodunum*. The remains of his theater once capable of holding 15,000 spectators survive, and so do two monumental Roman gateways, one of which was the model for the entrance gateway to the abbey in Cluny.

There was already a cathedral at Autun when Bishop Etienne decided to build a new one to house those valuable relics of St. Lazarus. Like so many prominent churchmen of his day the bishop held more than one position. He was also the abbot of Saulieu, a short distance to the north of Autun. With his strong ties to Cluny, Etienne had already commissioned sculptors from the Cluny work-shop to carve a series of wonderfully vigorous capitals for the Saulieu abbey church, many of which are still in existence in spite of re-peated ravages inflicted on the place over the succeeding centuries.

Gislebertus could have been working at Cluny as a young assistant at the time of the Saulieu commissions, between 1112 and 1113, and if so, it might well have been at this time that Etienne first became aware of the young man and his remarkable talent. In the ten or twelve years that followed Gislebertus's reputation would have continuously grown, so that by the time Bishop Etienne's revised plans for his new church at Autun took shape in about 1125 Gislebertus had become a man he was delighted to entrust with the task of carving the entire body of sculpture throughout the building.

The cathedral of St. Lazare is a gaunt and gray place crowded in among other gray buildings, and with none of the radiance and lightness of Vézelay. Perhaps because the architect was anxious to avoid any repetition of the roof collapsing as it had at Cluny, he made the walls sturdier by decreasing the number of windows, thereby reducing the light as well. And in reducing the light he made it well-nigh impossible for anyone to appreciate some of the most delightful carvings to be found anywhere: these are the fifty or more capitals which Gislebertus carved personally, representing scenes from the Old and New Testament. Fortunately for visitors today a number of these have been removed to the Chapter House, the originals having been replaced in the gloom of the nave by casts.

Here in the Chapter House they are a joy, carved with an extraordinary warmth and vitality, and every now and then with a taste for violence that is almost shocking. In the Flight to Egypt, Joseph seems to be singing cheerfully along the way, leading his obediently plodding donkey carrying a resigned Mary and baby Jesus on its back. The Dream of the Magi is one of the most enchanting and inventive of the capitals: the three kings are shown tucked up in the same narrow bed draped with a huge swathe of a coverlet whose folds are described with those delicate parallel lines. Each capital is like a page in an illustrated bible. Noah's Ark is like a dolls' house, with Noah's wife peering from the top window while two of the rescued animals gaze out of the window below her. Samson grasps a pillar of the temple carved in such a way that it seems literally to be collapsing around us. By contrast the three Magi bearing gifts to Bethlehem wear expressions of the most touching tenderness and wonder. And by further contrast the Fall of Simon Magus is described as pure horror, with the magician tumbling earthwards with a scream of terror as a winged and horned devil waits gleefully to claim his soul.

Gislebertus's world is one of constant and dramatic extremes between light and dark, between humor and pain, pathos and tragedy, combined always with that windblown movement of his figures suggested by the rippling folds of their garments.

The tympanum over the west door at Autun is his tour de force. The theme is the Last Judgment: the majestic figure of Christ is in the center, seated on a throne with his arms outstretched towards the damned on one side and the saved on the other. In 1766 the entire tympanum was considered an unsuitable relic of the age of superstition and was plastered over, to be replaced by a decoration so feeble and meaningless as to defy belief that anyone could have considered it to be a spiritual improvement. But at least the cathedral authorities retained enough respect for their heritage not to destroy the original tympanum, and ironically their act of prudishness served to save it from the iconoclastic mobs that vandalized so many churches and abbeys during the French Revolution only a few decades later. Eventually the tympanum was uncovered early in the nineteenth century, and duly restored in 1858 by that indomitable architect and passionate medievalist Viollet-le-Duc (some years after he had also restored Vézelay).

The Last Judgement was one of the most popular subjects in medieval church art; there must be thousands of them throughout Europe. But Gislebertus's figures are never clichés, and it is a measure of his genius that he could take such a well-worn convention and inject originality into every part of it. With a simple and moving gesture St. Peter reaches down with one hand to raise up the small and hopeful figure of a boy, while with the other hand he reassuringly holds up a colossal key to the gate of heaven. Nearby three naked children raise their arms in supplication to grasp the gentle figure of an angel. By contrast the devils on the other side of Christ are the most loathsome creatures imaginable, part-human, part-reptile, part-nightmare. And amid a lower frieze of figures the eye is suddenly caught by the image of a terrified creature about to be strangled by a pair of gigantic hands that have emerged, disembodied, from the shelf of stone above. This is surrealism many centuries before its time.

The tympanum is pieced together out of twenty-nine separate panels of stone, like a huge jigsaw. Many of the figures are greatly elongated, precursors of the famous carvings flanking the west door at Chartres made just a few decades later, though here at Autun these elongations may be a device by the sculptor to correct the steep perspective of figures who were designed to be seen from far below. Their slender limbs are caught up in that familiar swirling drapery that sweeps them along, often carved entirely in the round, freestanding against a wall of stone—an astonishing feat of skill, making it all the more remarkable that they have not been more damaged by centuries of weathering and the application of that covering of plaster in 1766. Only one fragment actually suffered— the head of Christ was deliberately removed, probably because it protruded too far for the plasterers to be able to cover it. Somehow the head found its way into the nearby Musée Rolin, where it was identified shortly after the Second World War and duly restored to its rightful place.

So the great tympanum above the west door of the cathedral became once again complete, just as it had been almost nine hundred years earlier when its creator had gazed with pride at so many years of work, and had celebrated that achievement with a display of justified vanity by signing his name in stone.

Surprisingly the west door was never used as the main entrance to the cathedral, contrary to the normal practice, apparently because it looked directly out over the city's principal burial ground. Instead, the congregation was required to enter by the north door. The authorities must have anticipated this novel arrangement because it was over the north door that Gislebertus was required to carve a second tympanum depicting the Raising of Lazarus, the saint to whom the new cathedral was dedicated.

The north tympanum no longer exists except in a few fragments, for reasons that would be comic had its loss been less tragic. Below the Raising of Lazarus Gislebertus carved a lintel spanning the entire width of the doorway; this was a horizontal frieze and it depicted the temptation of Adam in the Garden of Eden. The figure of Adam occupied the entire left-hand section of the lintel, while that of Eve, accompanied by the image of Satan in the form of a serpent, duly filled its right-hand space. Because of the broad width of the doorway the figures of Adam and Eve were close to life-size, and apart from a stray vine leaf or two both were entirely naked. However acceptable this full-frontal imagery was at the time, and presumably it was, six hundred years later such brazen sensuality was evidently too much for the cathedral authorities, and Gislebertus's second tympanum was torn down altogether by order of the cathedral chapter.

The few surviving fragments include four capitals on either side of the door, presumably considered harmless by the eighteenth-century religious censors. In addition there are a number of details that have turned up here and there. One particularly beautiful carving of an angel, with its garments swirling around its ankles as it appears to be flying across the face of the stone, found its way into the Metropolitan Museum of Art in New York, having previously been in the hands of a local priest who had presumably found it, or perhaps had rescued it from being smashed to pieces. Several further fragments are now preserved in Autun's Musée Rolin. One of these fragments is of the head and torso of a youth. Another, which had been built into the masonry of a house directly opposite the north doorway and discovered there as recently in 1907, depicts the Assumption of the Virgin Mary.

But of all the surviving fragments of Gislebertus's lost tympanum one carving stands out as among the most breathtaking masterpieces in all European sculpture—Eve. Gislebertus's Eve is the most striking single work of art bequeathed to us by what we can quite confidently describe as "the school of Cluny." She too was discovered by accident. In 1858 a house was pulled down that had been built a mere three years after the demolition of the north doorway. And there was Eve—she had been used as a building stone.

There has never been an image of Eve quite like this. In part the uniqueness of her lies in the way Gislebertus has utilized the shape of the stone in which she is carved. A lintel is long and narrow; hence both Eve and Adam needed to be horizontal and facing one another, head to head—hardly the conventional format

for illustrating the Temptation. We have no idea how Adam would have looked, but we can guess since we know precisely where he would have been in the composition. In the very center of the lintel is a slender tree which describes an S-shaped curve as it rises, so creating two concave spaces one above the other, one facing to the left, the other to the right. The lower of these spaces is now bare, but this is clearly where Adam's head once would have rested. No more than a few inches above it is the other space, and this is filled by the head of Eve. Her right hand is cupped beneath her chin as she whispers secretly to Adam while her other hand reaches behind her to pluck the forbidden fruit. It is a moment of conspiracy and seduction. Her long hair is combed rhythmically across her naked body, which is carved virtually in the round so that she reclines as though she were actually floating, weightless.

Perhaps it is no surprise that Autun's cathedral authorities should have found Eve's unashamed sensuality more than they could stomach. In traditional church iconography Eve was supposed to be a disobedient and manipulative creature responsible for man's downfall, a figure to despise and castigate. She was the Devil's handmaiden. But with Gislebertus there is no such moralizing. He shows us a woman whose sexuality is no longer the evil that cast mankind out of paradise, but rather a very human feature we are invited to appreciate and applaud. She represents the triumph of enjoyment over fear and superstition. She has become a creature to be celebrated. And in this way she transcends her medieval typecasting altogether, prefiguring the eventual passing of the Middle Ages with its unrelenting misogyny. She represents a turning point in art—a forerunner of that noble European tradition of the female nude, from Giorgione to Goya to Bonnard, Bernini to Maillol.

XVIII.

Decline and Fall

 Peter the Venerable died on Christmas Day, 1156. And with his death a curtain falls. He had been abbot of Cluny for thirty-four years—and it had been an eventful, at times heroic, period of office. In his eyes Cluny had been a precious treasury of the Christian Kingdom, and perhaps more than that, its very heart and soul—as if everything that was best about Christendom resided within its walls and within its empire.

It might seem that Peter had been clinging to the past for most of those thirty-four years, yet so long as the reins of power were firmly in his hands then that golden past had managed to live on. Universal respect for the man, even among Cluny's severest critics such as Bernard of Clairvaux, held back the tide of change.

But once he was no longer there the banks began to crumble. Elections that had once been unanimous (even when misguided as in the case of Abbot Pons) were now disputed; there were factions within the abbey. In the fifty years following Peter's death Cluny had no fewer than nine abbots, four more than over the previous two centuries! In part these disputes were symptomatic of a general relaxation of discipline within the abbey, a diminishing of that sense of common purpose and humble dedication that had always been one of the strengths of Cluny. Individual monks were becoming more vain and willful. Dependent abbeys caught the habit, too, no longer content to remain subject to the authority of the motherhouse in all things. Less than one year after the death of Abbot Peter the Emperor Frederick Barbarossa took the significant step of freeing Cluny's own motherhouse, Baume-les-Messieurs, from all subjection to the Burgundian abbey, confirming its independence and in consequence depriving Cluny of Baume's lands and possessions, and therefore of the income it had previously enjoyed from those possessions—including that immensely valuable commodity, salt.

The Cluniac empire was beginning to disintegrate. In 1162 the pope freed the wealthy abbey of Vézelay from Cluny, though the pontiff tactfully waited until after the death of its abbot, Peter the Venerable's younger brother.

Before long other great houses were shown the same path to independence: St.-Omer, St.-Honoré-les-Lerins, St.-Gilles, St. Jean d'Angély, Beaulieu, St.-Martial de Limoges, and many others. There were violent disturbances too, which shook the old abbey. In 1166 the nearby castle of Lourdon, which was a Cluniac property, was seized by the local count. When men from Cluny, presumably including monks, went to reclaim it from the interloper more than five hundred of them were "atrociously massacred like sheep" by the count's rabble army, according to the chronicler Hugh of Poitiers. At much the same time one of the short-term abbots of Cluny made a bid to correct what seems to have been a moral slide on the part of the citizens of the town by issuing a charter insisting that all adulterers be required to run naked through the streets. Clearly it was the custom that an abbot's authority extended well outside the walls of his abbey, or at least he assumed as much. There is no record of whether the townsfolk of Cluny actually complied with the abbot's charter, or simply went about their adulterous ways unabashed.

It has been claimed that a prime factor in Cluny's decline was spiritual exhaustion. It is undeniably true that the abbey's life of the spirit seems to have grown less bright and less urgent once its days of expansion were over. Cluny had become an institution rather than a force, dogged by a certain complacency to which all long-standing institutions are prone.

But there are other, more specific factors to be taken into account. When Cluny was founded early in the tenth century Christendom was in a fragile condition and feudal society was being shaped around it for mutual help and protection. The religious mood was dark, predictions of the Second Coming were rife. The state of the world seemed to justify the view that God was less than pleased with humankind. In consequence, throughout the church there was a morbid preoccupation with the Last Judgment and Divine Punishment. Into this life of shadows the Benedictine ideal offered a ray of light because it proposed a withdrawal from this evil world and a belief in the primacy of prayer. Cluny was a healing balm in a sick world.

Two and a half centuries later Christian Europe felt a different place—and religious thought had changed with it. Spiritual authority, as well as the energy that it generated, had to a great extent passed to the Cistercians. They were the ones who were now felt to be in tune with the times. Here was a vigorous and hard-working body of monks channeling their energies not into singing but into agriculture. They were turning wildernesses into profitable lands, and doing so by their own sweated labor—while the monks of Cluny maintained an army of lay brothers and laborers. The Cluniac passive obsession with hellfire and punishment seemed out of date, too, with the hieratic figure of Christ in Majesty forever seated in stern judgment surrounded by the saved and the damned. For the Cistercians the religious experience was of a different kind.

In their world we begin to sense a human Jesus and a human Virgin Mary as his mother. Expression of faith becomes something personal rather than corporate. In their daily religious life the emphasis is now on the individual—on a personal relationship with God, expressed in human rather than symbolic terms.

These humanist tendencies are already prefigured within the Cluniac world itself in the carvings of Gislebertus at Autun, and in those at Vézelay; they feel like a radical break from the past, with old Cluniac iconographic traditions being left behind. And in the following century these tendencies become even more pronounced in the figures decorating the portals of new Gothic cathedrals, in particular those of Chartres, Reims, Strasbourg, and Siena. The Cluniac vision had become yesterday's world.

Monastic life itself was also undergoing radical change. The emergence of the mendicant orders, principally the Franciscans (founded in 1209) and the Dominicans (1215), reversed the belief that religious communities needed to shun the sinful world. The Franciscan and Dominican friars saw it as their spiritual vocation to do precisely the opposite: armed with their vows of poverty and their rope sandals they stepped boldly into the wide and increasingly urban world. Prayers and fine works of art were no longer enough to rescue humankind from the eternal bonfire— action and direct help were now the order of the day. In this bustling new world the proud isolation of Cluny was beginning to appear as much a relic as the holy relics that were venerated in its churches.

❁

The changing fortunes of Cluny were to some extent masked by the manifest grandeur of the place. Towards the end of the twelfth century the entire abbey complex was enclosed by a wall, an impressive stone structure, parts of which still stand. And within this wall the material comfort both of monks and visitors was continually being improved over the following two centuries by the provision of fresh accommodation and amenities. Cluny was becoming a comfortable place to live—and to live free of expense and free of care. Both spiritual and physical welfare were amply provided; there was not even any requirement to work.

Then in the mid-fifteenth century came the first sign of overblown affluence. Until now the abbots of Cluny had occupied a relatively modest building known as the Palace of Pope Gelasius, though "palace" suggests something grander than it was. But when a wealthy aristocrat, Jean de Bourbon, became abbot in 1456 he had far loftier notions of an abbot's position in the world. He already held the post of bishop of Le Puy-en-Velay, but as a member of the family soon to become the French royal line he preferred to spend most of his time in Paris, at the seat of power. He was a cultured and gifted man as well as an able administrator: nevertheless, he saw his responsibilities at Cluny in rather different terms from those practiced by most of his predecessors. Jean de Bourbon managed to be in charge of the abbey without actually belonging to it. Accordingly, he purchased an area of land adjacent to the abbey gates and therefore separate from the main body of the abbey itself, and here he built a handsome residence appropriate for a man of his means and social standing. It was equipped with everything expected of a grand mansion: a guard-room for security, state as well as private apartments, vast public rooms for receptions, a kitchen large enough to feed any number of guests, as well as its own cloister and chapel. In other words, it was entirely independent of day-to-day abbey life. (Today this former abbot's palace houses the Musée d'Art et d'Archéologie.)

Even this degree of grandeur was not enough for his successor, Jacques d'Amboise, who became abbot in the year 1485. He proceeded to construct an even more splendid palace, partly Gothic and partly in the Italian Renaissance style, which managed to express its separateness from monastic affairs by turning its back on the entrance to the abbey. This second palace, known as the Palace of Jacques d'Amboise, which still stands most impressively, was built even more specifically to receive distinguished guests, and if the abbot still concerned himself with the Rule of St. Benedict it would only have been as an occasional break from leading the life of a courtier and playing host to the rich and famous.

But Cluny was not alone in its centuries-long decline. The Cistercian empire suffered a not dissimilar decay. Within fifty years of St. Bernard's death many of the abbeys he had helped to found had grown slack in discipline, a moral decline hastened in part by the order's phenomenal spiritual success and its consequent—yet ironic—accumulation of great wealth, all so totally at odds with its founder's stern ethic. Generally speaking the great age of the cloister gave way to the great age of the cathedral. Since the early Middle Ages the monasteries had been the spiritual and cultural heartland of Christendom, bulwarks against barbarism and anarchy, resolute guardians of the faith. But by the thirteenth century that heartland lay elsewhere, outside monastery walls, in the towns and cities where the friars of the new mendicant orders lived their poverty and their faith, where the new universities were beginning to open people's minds to wider regions of learning, and where a new

Gothic world was throwing up glorious cathedrals lifting the
human spirit to unimagined heights.

In the later Middle Ages the abbots of Cluny had decided that they
needed a residence in Paris. Nominally this was so that they could
visit the college which had been founded by the abbey close to the
Sorbonne. In reality it was because Paris was where they now spent
most of their time. A fourteenth-century abbot had already shown
some foresight by purchasing an area of land containing the ruins of
Roman baths situated at the crossing of what are now the
Boulevard St. Germain and the Boulevard St. Michel. And at the
end of the fifteenth century a handsome town residence was built
on the site, and here the new breed of absentee abbots enjoyed their
comfortable city existence far from Burgundy and even further
from the Rule of St. Benedict, in what became known as the Hôtel
de Cluny, and where at least one French monarch was welcomed as
a guest. (Today it has become the Musée de Cluny, a magnificent
museum of the Middle Ages, but retaining no connection
whatsoever with Cluny itself other than its name.)

The royal visit was no accident; the kings of France had come
to enjoy a commanding role in the life of Cluny. How this had
happened was more a case of sleight of hand than a crude royal
takeover. Cluny's long tradition of aristocratic control finally led the
abbey first into royal patronage and then into royal control. The
abbots themselves had by now become adjuncts of the royal court
and were only secondarily abbots of Cluny. It was little more than
a title, and a lucrative source of private income. The days when an
abbot was effectively the feudal lord of the monastery and its empire
were over. Within the Cluniac order generally authority was now

dispersed not just at Cluny itself but also in its dependent houses, which were decreasing in number almost year by year.

Of greater significance for the future of the abbey was that the monks had feebly allowed the traditional right to elect their own abbot to pass from their hands. That right was acquired in 1528 by the French king, who in consequence now effectively appropriated the abbey. Having once served God, it now served the monarch. Cluny had become a tool of the crown: a useful tool, as successive French rulers found the prestigious office of abbot of Cluny to be a most convenient gift to have in their possession. Francis I, patron of Leonardo da Vinci in his old age, had no qualms at all about appointing abbots (*abbés commendataires* or "commendatory abbots," as they were known) who had never even thought of taking monastic vows and who rarely deigned to visit the place, if they even knew where it was. The abbacy of Cluny had become purely a political appointment given as a reward for secular services to the French crown. It was, moreover, a highly lucrative reward, and a number of noble dynasties in France, notably the Guise family, feathered their nests most handsomely from the revenues which Cluny's estates continued to provide. These may have been fewer than in earlier centuries, but now that there were no more churches and priories to be built, or wars to fund, they were quite enough for high-born spendthrifts to enjoy.

The sixteenth-century wars of religion did Cluny no favors either. Even in its state of spiritual decline the abbey was still seen as a symbol of Catholic tyranny—perhaps even more so now that it was subject to royal authority. The place became a prime target for Protestant fury: the abbey was severely looted by Huguenots in 1562, and again twelve years later. The monks fled and sought refuge in the town, while in the course of the mayhem the magnificent library was looted and the greater part of it destroyed.

Sadly there is no record of what exactly was lost; certainly many of the finest illuminated manuscripts from the abbey's famous scriptorium perished.

But the abbey was not quite ready to die. A body of monks returned to repair what could be rescued from the pillage and to resume some semblance of a monastic life. Standards had by now slipped a great distance from those maintained with some strictness under Hugh the Great and Peter the Venerable. The rule of silence was no longer observed. Meat was eaten regularly, often in lavish quantities. Furthermore monks now insisted on enjoying individual bedrooms, rejecting the spartan discomfort of a common dormitory. In a belated moral rally the order split into two in 1621. The more sybaritic members were determined to retain the lax regime that had been allowed to creep in over the centuries (referred to ironically as *Ancienne Observance*, the former or old observance). In opposition to them were the more rigorous monks who strove to return to a form of discipline that came somewhere near the original Rule drawn up by St. Benedict. The latter group and their regime of *Étroite Observance* (strict observance) won the day, at least briefly. That they did so was largely due to the fact that in 1629 Cardinal Richelieu, the effective ruler of France, was appointed Cluny's abbot—or rather, he appointed himself. Richelieu held the post until 1642, and during those years took time off from running the country to impose long-overdue order and discipline on the abbey, and to restore some of its lost pride. For this Richelieu deserves credit. But in the process he decided to disband the entire order, enforcing its amalgamation with the relatively insignificant Order of St. Maur, which happened to be located conveniently close to Paris.

And so the life of the great abbey stumbled on, surviving further high-ranking political appointments as abbot—Cardinal Mazarin held the post from 1655 until his death six years later—as well as further indignities. By the middle of the eighteenth century only thirty-seven of its dependent monasteries remained under Cluny's wing, compared to the more than fifteen hundred in its heyday. Nonetheless, Mazarin received a reported annual stipend of 57,000 livres from tenure of the abbacy—an impressive sum, but less than the 140,000 livres he received from the royal abbey of Saint-Denis.

There was one last flourish—of a hollow kind. In 1750 the grand prior (rather more grand than he needed to be) decided to upgrade the monastery in accordance with the architectural taste of the time, which was heavily neoclassical. He noted the decayed condition of many of the surviving medieval areas of the abbey, but rather than restore them he chose to tear them down, replacing them with austere palatial buildings which preside drearily over what remains of Cluny today. He also added a vast and soulless cloister, designed in Paris.

The abbot at the time of Cluny's neoclassical buildings was a scion of the noble La Rochefoucauld family, a favorite of King Louis XV and a direct descendent of that eminent man of letters of the previous century, the Duc de la Rochefoucauld, author most famously of surgically sharp maxims, many of them directly towards men of power and pretension. As he gazed upon the massive but undistinguished new cloister and residential buildings being constructed by his grand prior, Abbot Frédéric-Jérôme de la Rochefoucauld might ruefully have recalled one of his ancestor's maxims: "Our virtues are usually only vices in disguise."

Frédéric-Jérôme's nephew succeeded him as abbot in 1757, and in an echo of Cluny's more heroic days Dominique de la Rochefoucauld remained abbot for over thirty years. But he was to be the last abbot of Cluny, swept away by the French Revolution. And the great church which Abbot Hugh had constructed became for a brief while the local parish church, even though it "could contain more than six times the entire population," according to a report by the Conseil Municipal.

The hurricane of political events in France was overtaking the little that remained of the doomed abbey, ensuring that even its fabric would soon fail to survive. The Bastille had fallen on July 14, 1789. In February 1790 the National Assembly ordered the suppression of all religious communities. Abbot de la Rochefoucauld, who was also a member of the Assembly, bravely voted against the resolution, after which he wisely fled to Germany. Being both an aristocrat and the head of a royal abbey he would have been doubly vulnerable. (He died in exile on September 25, 1800.) At the time of the suppression in 1790 there were forty-one monks left at Cluny. Of these six were guillotined, two continued a monastic life elsewhere, and the rest returned to a secular life. On October 25, 1791, in defiance of the dissolution of the abbey, a Mass was held at Cluny to mark the six hundredth anniversary of the consecration of the abbey church. A few monks managed to return briefly to celebrate the occasion.

A year later the French monarchy was overthrown. Cluny had now lost its only remaining protector. In Paris the slaughter of political prisoners, known as the September Massacres, followed; then in January 1793 Louis XVI was executed. In July the same year the Committee of Public Safety was formed under Robespierre, and the Reign of Terror began. More than a quarter of a million people—nobles and churchmen alike—were arrested on suspicion of being enemies of the Revolution, many of them then executed without trial or dying in prison. Revolutionary mobs began to descend on the abbey. In October a detachment of the Revolutionary Army stationed not far away at Chalon-sur-Saône was dispatched to Cluny specifically to vandalize the abbey buildings. What could not be burnt was blown up with gunpowder. At the same time all remaining Cluniac property throughout France was being confiscated; monasteries, priories, mills, salt mines, forests, vineyards, stables, and grazing land all became the property of the state, along with the handsome income which such property had yielded for so long.

Meanwhile the sheer vastness of the former abbey church rendered it a burden for the small secular community of Cluny to maintain, let alone to meet the cost of repairing the extensive damage caused by the revolutionary mobs. As a result, in July 1795 the place was declared redundant, and the more modest church of Notre Dame was deemed better suited to serve the needs of the local community. So, the greatest church in Christendom—forerunner of some of the most glorious architecture in Europe—was now abandoned, prey to the fates.

And the fates were less than kind. Three years later, in February 1798, a decree was issued by the local authorities permitting the church and remaining abbey buildings to be put up for sale in four separate lots. On April 21 of the same year all four lots were bought together for a little over two million francs by a syndicate of three speculators from Mâcon. One of the three, a Monsieur Gemillon, was an ex-priest. Another was a wealthy merchant by the name of Batonard who is said to have bribed the authorities with wine worth seven thousand francs. The third, a Monsieur Vacher, we know nothing about.

Their objective was clear—the ancient abbey was to become a stone quarry. And with more than two million francs at stake there was no time to waste; a demolition squad set to work immediately, beginning with the destruction of the western end of the church with its enormous carved portal on which the young Gislebertus may once have worked. This job duly completed with the aid of explosives, the new owners began to move eastwards, tearing down the vaulted roof and vast pillars of the church as they went, until they reached the fourth bay, at which point they decided to drive a broad road across the nave and side aisles at a higher level in order to create a useful link to the main street of the town, a road which soon became known as *la rue scélérate*—"Scoundrel Street."

Opposition to this mass destruction was not only local; it spread as far as Paris. Two years after the work of demolition had begun, but when much of the church was evidently still standing, the French government agreed to send a distinguished scholar, Alexandre Lenoir, to assess the situation and report back. This he did in no uncertain terms. "The church has the most beautiful nave in existence," he wrote. "This monument, famous for its antiquity and for its enormous size, is going to be destroyed from top to bottom; a greedy purchaser is having it demolished to sell as building material." Lenoir went on to explain that the citizens of the town deeply deplored what was going on, and were promising to restore it at their own cost if the present destruction could be halted. "Citizen Minister," he concluded. "I demand in the name of Art the conservation of this beautiful monument."

But Lenoir's demand fell on deaf ears, and the demolition of the abbey went on for a further eleven years. By this time all the main body of the church had been blown up and dragged away. Even the great set of bells, which had been cast in England almost seven hundred years earlier and donated to the abbey by the Empress Matilda, had been melted down for cannon. Then in 1809 the great central tower collapsed. And a year later the apse at the eastern end of the church was demolished to make room for a horses' stud farm. Utilitarianism had struck hard.

By the time the authorities finally called a halt to proceedings in the 1820s the three citizens of Mâcon were too gorged on their profits to feel much regret at not being allowed to finish the job that they had begun so industriously two decades earlier. In any case there was not much remaining for the demolition gangs to do. They left little behind them except what we see of Cluny today. What survived of the abbey, principally the neoclassical additions of 1750, was used as a school from 1866 onwards, and today the soulless cloister and other eighteenth-century buildings are home to the École Nationale Supérieure d'Arts et Métiers (ENSAM), specializing in new technologies.

The story goes that Napoleon, passing close by, refused to visit Cluny on the grounds that its inhabitants had perpetrated such vandalism. If true, the accusation is partly unjust; we know from Alexandre Lenoir's report to the French government that a sizeable number of the town's citizens were prepared to restore the abbey church at their own expense if only the demolition could be halted. It has also been claimed that by the end of the nineteenth century the very notion of there having once been an abbey at Cluny had been erased from people's minds. This too seems most unlikely; memories are not that feeble, and the legacy of a thousand years would hardly have evaporated in a mere three generations. Besides, we need only to look around at Cluny today. Much of the present town was actually built out of stone taken from the old abbey. Alongside handsome medieval houses which testify to the wealth which the abbey once brought to this place are numerous mansions that date from the period of the abbey's destruction. The stone was simply reused. Furthermore, a number of these mansions display carvings carefully set into the walls, or over doorways—heraldic crests, figures, geometrical motifs, floral patterns. Where they came from is no mystery. All these carved stones would once have graced some area of the old abbey, either bought or stolen when the demolition gangs were in operation.

However many tears may have been shed as the townsfolk witnessed the demolition of their abbey, clearly those three entrepreneurs from Mâcon did a roaring local trade in monastic artefacts—and like the jackdaws that today clack and clatter over the town, there must have been plenty of citizens of Cluny who swarmed over the body of the abbey plucking out the jewels of the place and carrying them proudly away.

The search for Cluny ends where it began. We depart through the monumental gateway with its echoes of imperial Rome, and follow the ghost of Abbot Hugh's great church through the streets of the old town that was built of its stones. We can take a skeptical view of its downfall and maintain that the tragedy of Cluny lay in allowing itself to be seduced by the material world, until that material world repaid the compliment by consuming it, stone by stone.

Or we can take a broader view and say that what Cluny bequeathed to European civilization stands before us in the form of some of the greatest church architecture and carving we have, from Vézelay and Autun to Chartres and Canterbury, and that what it achieved in its heyday is well worthy of the description awarded it by Pope Urban II in the eleventh century:

"Cluny shines as another sun over the earth."

Bibliography

Allsopp, B., *Romanesque Architecture* (London, 1971)

Armi, C.E., *Masons and Sculptors in Romanesque Burgundy: The New Aesthetic of Cluny III* (University Park, PA, 1983)

Aubert, M., *French Sculpture at the Beginning of the Gothic Period* (Paris, 1929)

Barlow, F., *William I and the Norman Conquest* (London, 1965);
    The Norman Conquest and Beyond (London, 1983)

Barraclough, G. (ed), *Eastern and Western Europe in the Middle Ages* (London, 1970);
    The Crucible of Europe (London, 1976)

Beckwith, J., *Early Mediaeval Art* (London, 1964)

Benson, R.L., and Constable, G., (eds), *Renaissance and Renewal in the Twelfth Century* (Oxford, 1982)

Benton, J., *Self and Society in Mediaeval France* (Toronto, 1984)

Berlioz, J., *Saint Bernard en Bourgogne—Lieux et Mémoires* (Paris, 1990)

Bouchard, C.B., *Sword, Mitre and Cloister: Nobility and the Church in Burgundy, 980-1198* (Ithaca, NY, and London, 1987)

Braunfels, W., *Monasteries of Western Europe* (London, 1972)

Bredero, A.H., *Bernard of Clairvaux: Between Cult and History* (Edinburgh, 1996)

Brooke, C.N.L., *Europe in the Central Middle Ages* (London, 1964);
    The Twelfth-Century Renaissance (London, 1969);
    The Structure of Mediaeval Society (London, 1971);
    The Monastic World (London, 1974);
    The Mediaeval Idea of Marriage (Oxford, 1989);
    The Age of the Cloister (Mahwah, NJ, 2003)

Brundage, J.A., *Law, Sex and Christian Society* (Chicago, 1987)

Bullough, V.L., and Brundage, J.A., (eds), *Handbook of Mediaeval Sexuality* (London, 1996)

Burge, J., *Héloïse and Abelard: A Twelfth-Century Love Story* (London, 2003)

Clanchy, M.T., *Abelard: A Mediaeval Life* (Oxford, 1997)

Coleman, J., *Ancient and Mediaeval Memories* (Cambridge, 1992)

Conant, K.J., *Carolingian and Romanesque Architecture* (London, 1959);
    Cluny, les Églises et la Maison du Chef d'Ordre (Mâcon, 1968)

Constable, G. (ed), *The Letters of Peter the Venerable* (Cambridge, 1967);
    Cluniac Studies (London, 1980);
    The Reformation of the Twelfth Century (Cambridge, 1996);
    Cluny from the Tenth to the Twelfth Centuries (Aldershot, 2000);

Cowdrey, H.E.J., *The Cluniacs and the Gregorian Reform* (Oxford, 1970)

Daniel-Rops, H., *Bernard of Clairvaux* (New York, 1964)

Deanesly, M., *A History of the Mediaeval Church* (London, 1969)

Deschamps, P., *French Sculpture of the Romanesque Period* (Paris, 1930)

Dronke, P., *Abelard and Héloïse in Mediaeval Testaments* (Glasgow, 1976);
    A History of Twelfth-Century Western Philosophy (Cambridge, 1988)

Dubois, J., *Les Ordres Monastiques* (Paris, 1985)

Dunlop, I., *Burgundy* (London, 1990)

Evans, G., *Anselm* (London, 1987)

Evans, J., *Monastic Life at Cluny* (Oxford, 1931);
　　The Romanesque Architecture of the Order of Cluny (Cambridge, 1938);
　　Art in Mediaeval France (London, 1948);
　　Cluniac Art of the Romanesque Period (Cambridge, 1950);
　　Dress in Mediaeval France (Oxford, 1952);
　　Life in Mediaeval France (London, 1969)

Focillon, H., *Art of the West in the Middle Ages,* Vol. 2 (London, 1963)

Garrigou Grandchamp, P. (& others), *La Ville de Cluny et ses Maisons (XIe-XVe Siècles)* (Paris, 1997)

Gardner, A., *Mediaeval Sculpture in France* (Cambridge, 1931)

Gervers, M. (ed), *The Second Crusade and the Cistercians* (New York, 1992)

Gilson, E., *The Mystical Theology of St. Bernard* (Kalamazoo, MI, 1940)

Gunn, P., *Burgundy: Landscape with Figures* (London, 1976)

Haseldine, J.(ed), *Friendship in Mediaeval Europe* (Stroud, 1999)

Haskins, C.H., *The Renaissance of the Twelfth Century* (Cambridge, MA, 1928)

Hunt, N., *Cluny under Saint Hugh, 1049-1109* (London, 1967);
　　(ed), *Cluniac Monasticism in the Central Middle Ages* (London, 1971)

Iogna–Prat, D., *Order and Exclusion: Cluny and Christendom Face Heresy, Judaism and Islam* (Ithaca, NY and London, 2002)

Johnson, P., *Equal in Monastic Profession: Religious Women in Medieval France* (Chicago, 1991)

Kapelle, W.E., *The Norman Conquest of the North* (London, 1979)

Kenny, A., *The God of the Philosophers* (Oxford, 1979)

Ker, W.P., *The Dark Ages* (London, 1904)

Knight, G.R., *The Correspondence between Peter the Venerable and Bernard of Clairvaux* (Aldershot, 2002)

Knowles, D., *The Religious Orders in England* (Cambridge, 1948);
　　Saints and Scholars, 25 Mediaeval Portraits (Cambridge, 1962);
　　The Evolution of Mediaeval Thought (London, 1962);
　　The Monastic Order in England (Cambridge, 1963);
　　"Cistercians and Cluniacs: The Controversy between St. Bernard and Peter the Venerable," in *The Historian and Character, and Other Essays* (Cambridge, 1963);
　　Christian Monasticism (London, 1969);
　　Mediaeval Religious Houses, England and Wales (London, 1971)

Kritzeck, J., *Peter the Venerable and Islam* (Princeton, 1964)

Lang, A.P., "The Friendship Between Peter the Venerable and Bernard of Clairvaux," in *Bernard of Clairvaux; Studies Presented to Dom J. Leclercq* (Washington, 1973)

Leclercq, Dom J., *Pierre le Vénérable* (Abbey of St. Wandrille, France, 1946);
　　Bernard of Clairvaux (Paris, 1989)

Leff, G., *Mediaeval Thought* (London, 1958)

Lekai, L.J., *The Cistercians, Ideals and Reality* (Columbus, OH, 1977)

Lougnot, C., *Cluny: Pouvoir de l'An Mille* (Paris, 1987)

Loyn, H.R., *The Norman Conquest* (London, 1982)

Luscombe, D., *The School of Peter Abelard* (Cambridge, 1969);
　　Peter Abelard (London, 1979)

Marenbon, J., *The Philosophy of Peter Abelard* (Cambridge, 1997)

Marguey-Melin, B., *La Destruction de l'Abbaye de Cluny 1789-1823* (Cluny, 1985)

McLeod, E., *Héloïse, a Biography* (London, 1938)

Mews, C.J., *The Lost Love Letters of Heloise and Abelard* (Basingstoke, 1999);
    Abelard and His Legacy (Aldershot, 2001)

Mullins, E., *The Pilgrimage to Santiago* (London, 1974, Oxford, Signal, 2001);
    The Painted Witch (London, 1985)

Murray, A.V., *Abelard and St. Bernard* (Manchester, 1967)

Oldenbourg, Z., *St. Bernard* (Paris, 1970)

Oursel, R., *L'Art de Bourgogne* (Paris, 1953);
    Romanesque (London, 1967)

Pacaut, M., *L'Ordre de Cluny* (Paris, 1986)

Pernoud, R.M.J., *The Glory of the Mediaeval World* (London, 1950);
    Héloïse and Abelard (London, 1973)

Pevsner, N., *An Outline of European Architecture* (London, 1948)

Phillips, J., *Defenders of the Holy Land* (Oxford, 1996)

Pignot, J.-H., *Histoire de l'Ordre de Cluny depuis la Fondation de l'Abbaye jusqu'à la
    Mort de Pierre le Vénérable* (Autun, 1868)

Pirenne, H., *Economic and Social History of Mediaeval Europe* (trans, London, 1936);
    A History of Europe (trans, London, 1939);
    Mohammed and Charlemagne (trans, London, 1939)

Porter, A.K., *The Romanesque Sculpture of the Pilgrimage Roads* (Boston, 1923)

Rashdall, H., *Universities of Europe in the Middle Ages,* 3 vols., (Oxford, 1936)

Robertson, D.W., *Abelard and Héloïse* (New York, 1972)

Rosenwein, B., *Rhinoceros Bound: Cluny in the Tenth Century* (Philadelphia, 1982)

Rudolph, C., *The "Things of Greater Importance": Bernard of Clairvaux's Apologia and
    the Medieval Attitude towards Art* (Philadelphia, 1990)

Scott James, B., *St. Bernard of Clairvaux* (London, 1937)

Southern, R.W., *The Making of the Middle Ages* (Oxford, 1953);
    Mediaeval Humanism and Other Essays (London, 1970)

Starkie, W., *The Road to Santiago* (London, 1957)

Stratford, N. (with Saulnier, L.), *La Sculpture Oubliée de Vézélay: Catalogue du Musée
    Lapidaire* (Geneva, 1984);
    (ed), *Romanesque and Gothic: Essays for George Zarnecki* (Woodbridge,
    Suffolk, 1987)

Timmers, J.J.M., *A Handbook of Romanesque Art* (London, 1969)

Trevor-Roper, H., *The Rise of Christian Europe* (London, 1966)

Vielliard, J., *Le Guide du Pélérin de Saint-Jacques de Compostelle* (trans from 12th cent
    Latin, Mâcon, 1969)

Wadell, H., *Peter Abelard* (London, 1933)

West, T.W., *History of Architecture in France* (London, 1969)

Wheeler, B. (ed), *Listening to Heloise: The Voice of a Twelfth-Century Woman*
    (New York, 2000)

Zarnecki, G. (with Grivot, D.), *Gislebertus, Sculptor of Autun* (Paris and
    London, 1961);
    The Monastic Achievement (London, 1972)

Index

Abbeville abbey 148
Abbot Hugh's Hostelry 95
Abelard, Peter 155, 196-205
Achard of Montmerle 99
Adam 10, 217, 218, 219
Adelaide, Empress 47
Alcuin 24
Alfonso VI, King 74, 75, 76, 80, 107, 108, 121, 147, 161
Alfonso VII, King 161
Anselm 104
Anzy-le-Duc church 119, 123
Aquinas, Thomas 8, 200
Archambaud of Bourbon 45
Astrolabe 198
Auch 70
Autun 3, 47, 120, 123, 209, 211, 213; St. Lazare cathedral 154, 205, 207, 208-210, 212, 213, 214-219
Ava 15
Aymard, Abbot 25, 26

Barabans, Les 3, 118
Barbarossa, Frederick, Emperor 222
Baume-les-Messieurs monastery 13, 18, 44, 116, 159, 160, 222
Beatus 153
Beaulieu abbey 222
Bec-Hellouin abbey 103, 104
Benedict of Nursia 9, 22, 67, 113, 172, 176, 193, 229; Benedictine order 9, 22, 51, 95, 124; Rule of St. Benedict 9, 22, 23, 29, 44, 52, 53, 66, 83, 134-136, 143, 168, 172, 176, 178, 195, 226, 227
Bernard of Clairvaux 137, 155, 167-177, 179-182, 185, 189-190, 196, 201-204, 221
Bernard of Morlaix 158
Bernard of Uxelles 133
Bernay 103

Berno, Abbot 13-15, 16, 17, 18, 19, 26, 46, 94, 95
Berzé-la-Ville 93, 94, 95, 126
Bibliothèque Nationale 126, 142
Blanot 41-42
Bois-Sainte-Marie church 124
Bonaparte, Napoleon 234
Bourbon, Jean de 225
Bourges 16, 133
Brancion 110, 111, 112, 194
Brionnais 120, 122, 123, 124

Caen 101, 104
Canossa 85, 88, 89, 90
Carrión de los Condes 161
Chalon-sur-Saône 62, 204, 231
Chapaize 35, 194
Chapelle des Moines 93, 94, 95, 126
Charlemagne, Emperor 7, 15, 24, 29, 63, 64, 85
Charlieu church 119, 124
Châteauneuf church 123, 124
Cistercian order 79, 155, 156, 159, 167-172, 174, 175, 176, 177, 178, 181, 223, 226
Citeaux 168, 173, 196
Clairvaux 169, 171
Clermont 98, 99
Clocher de l'Eau Bénite 4, 117, 118
Clocher des Bisans 118
Clocher des Lampes 118
Clocher du Choeur 118
Cluny
    administration of 51, 109, 157
    and *Ancienne Observance* 229
    architecture 26-27, 116-119
    autonomy of 16, 21, 50
    and book illustration 125, 142
    Cluny I 18, 26
    Cluny II 26-27, 40, 75
    Cluny III 27, 76, 116, 117, 119, 129, 151, 157, 184, 188, 207

and Crusades 97–101, 107, 146, 179, 180
daily life 66, 129–143
decline 221–224, 228, 229, 230
destruction of 232–234
donations to 31, 46, 47–49, 50, 51, 71, 98, 100, 107–109, 128, 140, 147, 156, 189
and England 69, 104, 105, 106, 107, 127, 183, 187–189
and *Étroite Observance* 229
and ENSAM 234
founding 14–18
and French Revolution 231–233
influence of 17, 45, 46, 49, 63, 73, 76, 79, 89, 96, 104, 109, 167, 188
and Italy 89
and monastic reform 44, 51, 104, 171, 137
and music 11, 18, 27, 49, 125, 167
and nuns 70, 193–195
and oblates 48, 134
opposition to 50, 67, 108, 110, 168–176, 221–223
Order of Cluny 51
and Order of St. Maur 229
Pax Dei 46
and painting 94–95
and scriptorium 125, 130, 141, 142, 176
and sculpture 5, 11, 120, 122–124, 125, 167
and Spain 53–56, 70, 72–77, 108, 127, 145
and town 3, 4, 5, 110, 140, 233, 234, 235
and wine 22, 95, 110–111, 126, 130, 131, 134, 136, 140, 158
Conant, Kenneth John 27, 117, 119, 207
Córdoba 53, 55
Cosimir of Poland 132
Crusade, First 53, 97, 98, 99, 100, 101, 107, 184
Crusade, Second 169, 179, 180, 181
Cruzille 112, 113

D'Amboise, Jacques 226
Dalmatius, Count 60, 61, 62
Damian, Peter 49, 142
Dark Ages 16
De Warenne, William 105, 106
Dominican order 224
Donation of Constantine 84

Eauze 70
El Cid 72, 74
Estella 161
Etienne, Bishop of Autun 209, 210, 213, 214
Eudes de Bourgougne 77
Evans, Joan 95
Eve 10, 218–219

Farges 34
Fécamp 103
Ferdinand I, King 73, 74
Feudalism 19, 20, 45
Figeac 70
Flying buttresses 184
Francis I, King 228
Franciscan order 224
Fulbert, Bishop 45
Fulbert, Canon 197, 198

Gigny monastery 19
Gilo 104, 105, 146
Gislebertus 205, 208, 209, 210–219, 224, 232
Glaber, Raoul 14, 15, 38–43, 52, 56, 121
Gorze monastery 171
Gothic architecture 43, 174, 224, 226, 227
Grande Chartreuse, La 173
Grivot, Abbé 210
Grosne, River 13, 42, 94, 191
Guillot, Alain 112, 113
Guiscard, Robert 91, 101
Gunzo 116
Guy II, Count of Mâcon 132

Harding, Stephen 168
Harpin, Eudes 133

Héloïse 196, 197, 198, 199, 200, 204, 205
Henry I, King of England 183-189
Henry I, King of France 60
Henry II, Emperor 47, 50
Henry II, King 191
Henry III, Emperor 64, 65, 85
Henry IV, Emperor 65, 80, 82, 85-90, 97
Henry V, Emperor 186
Henry VIII, King 187
Henry of Blois 188-192
Hezelon of Liège 116
Hirsau abbey 171
Holy Roman Empire 15
Hôtel de Cluny 227
Hugh, Abbot (St. Hugh) 43, 59-66, 69-77, 79-83, 85, 86, 88, 89, 90, 91, 93-99, 101, 104-109, 111, 112, 113, 115-117, 119, 120, 121, 124, 126-128, 129, 130, 131, 132, 137, 145, 146, 149, 159, 170, 175, 183, 193, 212, 230, 235
Hugh II, Abbot 149
Hugh of Vermondois 101

Islam 53, 56, 72, 97, 121, 162-165

Jerusalem 23, 71, 97, 99, 101, 181
John of Salerno 18, 22, 23
Jolivet, Abbé 95
Jumièges 103

La Charité-sur-Loire priory 69, 185
Lampert of Hersfeld 87-89
Lancharre priory 194, 195
Landry of Nevers 45
Lanfranc 104, 105
La Rochefoucauld, Dominique de, Abbot 230, 231
La Rochefoucauld, Frédéric-Jérôme de, Abbot 230
Lenoir, Alexandre 233, 234
Le Puy 101, 161
Le Thoronet abbey 174
Leyrac 70
Limoges 70, 222

Lombardy 29, 30, 31
Louis VII, King 179
Louis the Pious 24
Lund cathedral 30

Mâcon 2, 13, 15, 32, 41, 95, 113, 230, 232, 235
Magistri comacini 29
Mainz cathedral 30
Marcigny nunnery 69, 98, 124, 132, 193, 194
Martellange, Father 184
Matilda of Tuscany, Countess 88, 89, 90
Matilda, Queen 118, 185
Matilda, Empress 186, 187, 190, 191, 233
Mayeul, Abbot 25, 26, 27, 29, 30, 37, 38, 40, 43, 103, 120, 175
Mazarin, Cardinal 229
Mazille 42
Mesvres monastery 47
Millennium 34, 37, 38
Moissac 70, 151-154, 161
Montboissier, Pierre de 149, 212
Montceaux-l'Etoile church 123
Monte Cassino monastery 22, 23, 24, 25, 37, 67, 148
Mont-St.-Michel 103
Mont-St.-Vincent 40, 41, 119
Musée d'Art et d'Archéologie 6, 118, 211, 225
Musée de Cluny, Paris 227
Musée du Farinier 5, 118, 119, 122, 207, 210
Musée Lapidaire, Vézelay 212
Musée Rolin, Autun 216, 218

Nájera 161
Noirmoutier monastery 33
Normandy 15, 81, 103, 104, 188
Notre Dame priory, La Charité 69

Ochier, Dr. 6
Odilo, Abbot (St. Odilo) 38, 43-45, 47, 49, 50, 51-55, 57, 62, 72, 73, 132, 151, 155, 175
Odo, Abbot 18-19, 21-24, 25, 125, 175

Osbert 160
Otto I, Emperor 47
Otto II, Emperor 26

Palace of Pope Gelasius 225
Pamplona 53, 161
Paraclete, The 199, 204, 205
Paray-le-Monial 120, 121, 123
Paternus 56
Peter the Venerable, Abbot 149-151,
    155-165, 167, 169, 170, 172, 175-
    182, 183, 185, 188, 190, 191, 196,
    201, 203, 204, 212, 221, 222, 229
Philip I, King 80, 101
Plantagenet, Geoffrey 186
Pons, Abbot 145-151, 157, 161, 177,
    221
Pope Anacletus II 155
Pope Calixtus II 115, 148
Pope Clement III 90, 97
Pope Eugenius III 159, 171, 172
Pope Gregory VII 76, 80-91, 97, 111
Pope Innocent II 77, 116, 155, 157, 202
Pope John XI 21
Pope John XIX 50
Pope Leo IX 63, 64, 65, 85
Pope Paschal II 145
Pope Urban II 2, 6, 92, 96, 97, 98, 99,
    101, 108, 115, 119, 159, 235
Puente la Reina 75

Qur'an 163, 164

Raimondo, Archbishop of Toledo 162
Raymond of Saint-Gilles 101
Reading abbey 100, 186, 187
Reconquest of Spain 44, 53-54, 70,
    72, 74, 115
Renaud de Semur 212
Richard I, Duke of Normandy 103
Richard II, Duke of Normandy 103
Richelieu, Cardinal 229
Rievaulx abbey 174
Robert of Ketton 164
Robert II, Duke of Normandy 184
Robert II of Flanders 101
Romainmotier monastery 46

Romanesque architecture 28-29, 30,
    40, 41, 119, 207, 212
Rome 21, 23, 24, 29, 63, 64, 76, 82,
    83, 84, 85, 90, 91, 96, 97, 101, 104,
    105, 111, 133, 148, 150, 155, 169,
    177, 203, 235
Roncesvalles 161

Sacré-Coeur, Basilique du 120
Sahagún abbey 75, 76, 161
St. Bénigne monastery 29, 40
St. Benoît abbey 22
St. Blaise church 42
St. Gilles abbey 70, 222
St. Honoré-les-Lerins abbey 222
St. James 23, 53, 70-72, 100, 161, 186,
    187
St. Jean d'Angély 70, 222
St. Julien-de-Jonzy church 123, 124
St. Martial de Limoges abbey 222
St. Marcel monastery 62, 204
St. Martin church 35
St. Martin-des-Champs priory 69
St. Martin du Canigou monastery 30
St. Omer abbey 222
St.-Ouen abbey 103
St. Pancras priory 105
St. Paul 17, 41, 63, 66, 113, 153
St. Peter 16, 17, 32, 41, 63, 66, 74, 94,
    100, 113, 216
St. Peter's, Rome 1, 90, 174, 203
St. Philibert church 32-34
St. Victor monastery 48
St.-Wandrille abbey 103
Saintes 70
Sancho II, King 74
Sancho III, King 55, 56, 73
San Juan de la Peña monastery 56
San Michele de Locedia abbey 28
Sant'Apollinare in Classe
    monastery 47
Santiago de Compostela 23, 53, 70-72,
    74, 75 146, 161, 186
Saône, river 15, 32, 41
Saône-et-Loire *département* 3, 40
Saracens 7, 15, 26, 37, 99, 164
Saulieu abbey 213

Sauxillanges abbey 45, 46, 98, 178
Semur-en-Brionnais 60, 61, 69, 124
Sens cathedral 202
Serrabonne monastery 30
Souvigny abbey 46, 98
Speyer cathedral 30
Stephen, King 189
Stone vaulting 31
Stratford, Neil 212

Toledo 76, 162
Toulouse 70, 100
Tournus 32, 33, 34, 35, 41, 42,
    52, 110

Uchizy 34
Urraca 75

Varenne l'Arconce church 124
Vézelay abbey 47, 120, 123, 154, 169,
    179, 180, 205, 207, 212-213, 214,
    215, 222, 224, 235
Viollet-le-Duc 215
Vitalis, Orderic 157

William of St. Thierry 175
William of Volpiano 28, 29, 30, 40, 103
William the Conqueror 16, 60, 81,
    104, 106, 118, 183, 186
William I of Aquitaine, Duke 13-18,
    19, 46, 49, 94
William II, King 184
Winchester 184, 188, 189, 190, 191, 192

Zarnecki, George 210, 211, 212, 213

List of Illustrations

The illustrations are by Nicki Averill & Debbie Thorne.

Page 1: The Holy Water Belfry, Cluny

Page 10: Detail from a Last Judgment

Page 13: A medieval knight

Page 23: St. Benedict

Page 25: St. Philibert, Tournus

Page 34: St. Martin, Chapaize

Page 37: The church at Blanot

Page 54: The Great Mosque (Mezquita) in Córdoba

Page 59: Detail from the consecration of Cluny's new altar by Pope Urban II in 1095

Page 62: The castle in Semur

Page 69: A pilgrim on the road to Santiago

Page 76: Sahagún

Page 79: Emperor Henry IV

Page 89: Abbot Hugh, Emperor Henry IV, and Countess Matilda of Tuscany at Canossa

Page 93: Berzé-la-Ville

Page 103: William the Conqueror

Page 110: A Romanesque house in Cluny

Page 115: Cluny III, view of the choir (reconstructive drawing)

Page 119: Cluny III, the main nave (reconstructive drawing)

Page 129: A Cluniac monk

Page 142: Detail from an illuminated manuscript

Page 145: The cloister, Moissac

Page 153: The apostle Paul, Moissac

Page 155: Monks in procession

Page 167: Bernard of Clairvaux

Page 178: Detail from a capital, Cluny

Page 183: Flying buttress

Page 189: Henry of Blois

Page 193: Lancharre priory

Page 199: Abelard and Héloïse

Page 207: Detail from the tympanum, Vézelay

Page 218: The Eve of Autun

Page 221: Cluny in ruins

Page 226: The palace of Abbot Jacques d'Amboise